THE PC ANSWER BOOK

by Pat Barrett

alpha books

A Division of Prentice Hall Computer Publishing
11711 North College, Carmel, Indiana 46032 USA

International Standard Book Number: 0-672-30227-6
Library of Congress Catalog Card Number: 92-72903

95 94 93 92   8 7 6 5 4 3 2 1

Interpretation of the printing code: the rightmost number of the first series of numbers is the year of the book's printing; the rightmost number of the second series of numbers is the number of the book's printing. For example, a printing code of 92-1 shows that the first printing of the book occurred in 1992.

Printed in the United States of America

Special thanks to Hilary J. Adams for assuring the technical accuracy of this book.

Marie Butler-Knight
Publisher

Elizabeth Keaffaber
Managing Editor

Lisa A. Bucki
Product Development Manager

Susan Orr Klopfer
Acquisitions/Development Editor

Linda Hawkins
Senior Production Editor

Albright Communications, Incorporated, and San Dee Phillips
Manuscript Editors

Raymond E. Werner
Consulting Writer

Bill Hendrickson
Cover and Interior Designer

Steve Vanderbosch
Illustrator

Hilary J. Adams
Indexer

Mark Enochs, Tim Groeling, Carla Hall-Batton, John Kane, Carrie Keesling, Michele Laseau, Linda Quigley, Angie Trzepacz, Kelli Widdifield, Allan Wimmer
Production Team

For my mother, who encouraged me to read
My father, who encouraged my curiosity
And Patti, who simply encouraged me

Pat Barrett, writer, is an engineer who likes to motorcycle around the Pacific Northwest. He also likes to ski on land and water. Pat enjoys his two pet birds.

Steve Vanderbosch, artist, doesn't have any pets and really likes to go on vacations—especially in the Virgin Islands. He also likes to snow ski, bike ride, and swim.

Contents

Help! Table

Many common problems facing people who use PCs are listed in this table, along with page references. Look for the chapter that matches your problem area, then scan the listed problems for one that matches or is close to your problem, and you'll see a corresponding page number. Many problems will list several solutions. Also, each chapter has additional information that could be helpful to you.

Chapter 3 Problems with Cables and Connectors

Problem: I turned my computer on, but nothing happens. See page 27.

Problem: I just turned on my computer and my mouse isn't working. See page 28.

Problem: My printer is turned on, and its lights are lit, but when I try to print a file, nothing happens, or I get an error message that says something like "Errors on list device indicate that it may be off-line. Please check it." See page 29.

Problem: My old cable does not fit my new printer. See page 29.

Problem: I tried to attach my new gee-whiz video monitor to my computer and found that the connectors don't match. See page 30.

Problem: My external modem is not working correctly. See page 30.

Problem: My internal modem is not working correctly. See page 31.

Problem: My computer has a SCSI port but it doesn't recognize some or all of the devices (printers, etc.) connected to the port. See page 32.

Problem: My computer cannot find its external hard disk. It won't boot properly. See page 33.

Chapter 4 Problems with Disks and Disk Drives

Problem: My PC won't read my diskette. It's giving me a message that says "Invalid media." See page 36.

Problem: My PC won't boot. My screen is telling me "Non-system disk or disk error, Replace and press any key when ready," or "Bad or missing Command Interpreter." See page 38.

Problem: It seems to take a long time to read and write files to my hard drive. My machine used to do that much faster. See page 41.

Problem: My PC reports a sector not found when it tries to read a floppy diskette. See page 42.

Problem: I put my diskette in a friend's machine and got the dread sector-not-found error message. See page 42.

Problem: My PC occasionally gives the sector-not-found message when reading my hard drive, but then it finds other files. See page 43.

Problem: I ran CHKDSK and it reports lost chains or clusters. See page 44.

Problem: The diskettes in my disk drive become hot during use. See page 45.

Chapter 5 Problems with Keyboards

Problem: EVERYTHING I TYPE IS IN CAPITAL LETTERS! HOW CAN I GET BACK TO lowercase letters? See page 49.

Problem: My arrow keys make numbers on my screen instead of moving the cursor. See page 49.

Problem: My keyboard is dead. See page 50.

Problem: My keyboard is still dead. See page 50.

Problem: I tried another keyboard, which also didn't work. See page 51.

Chapter 7 Telecommunications and Problems with Ports

Problem: I have been told by one person to connect my printer to the printer port, and by another to connect it to a parallel port. What are they, and what's the difference between them? See page 70.

Problem: What's a serial port? A communication port? See page 70.

Problem: What are COM1 and COM2? See page 70.

Problem: How many serial or COM ports does my PC have? See page 71.

Problem: I have a mouse, a scanner and have now purchased a modem. I need to have a third serial port; how do I do it? See page 72.

Problem: My scanner installation instructions tell me to select an interrupt, or IRQ. What what are they, and should I care about them? See page 72.

Problem: My mouse is connected to a serial port, and it's not working. See page 73.

Problem: The setup instructions for my telecommunications hardware talk about DTE and DCE. What are they? See page 74.

Problem: The telecommunications software wants me to select a terminal emulation. What's that and what should I choose? See page 74.

Problem: My telecommunications software is asking for a baud rate (or "BPS"). Which value should I choose? See page 75.

Problem: OK, now my telecommunications software wants to know what parity I want. See page 77.

Problem: My telecommunications software is asking me to select the number of stop bits. See page 78.

Problem: I've done everything I'm supposed to, and my modem still doesn't work. See page 78.

Problem: How can I really tell if my modem is working properly? See page 79.

Problem: I get the OK, now how do I make my modem dial the telephone? See page 80.

Problem: My modem has just stopped working. See page 81.

Problem: What's a "host mode"? What's an "auto-answer mode"? See page 81.

Problem: I want to download a file from a bulletin board. What protocol should I use? See page 81.

Problem: How can I make my modem hang up the phone? See page 82.

Chapter 8 Problems with Printers and Fonts

Problem: My software manual says that I need to have an IBM-compatible printer. How do I find out if I do? See page 86.

Problem: I can't locate my printer's switches. See page 87.

Problem: I don't understand my printer's switch settings. See page 88.

Problem: My printer is not printing, printing oddly, or printing garbage. See page 90.

Problem: My printer will not print. See page 90.

Problem: My printer is beeping at me. See page 91.

Problem: My printer is printing in the wrong place on each page. See page 92.

Problem: I need to tell my software where to find my printer (what port it is on). How can I find out? See page 93.

Problem: Whenever I try to print anything my computer says "Bad command or filename." See page 95.

Problem: I want to print a file but my PC reports "File not found." See page 97.

Problem: My computer keeps asking me for the "Name of list device [PRN]." See page 98.

Problem: I want to print what's on my computer screen. How do I do it? See page 99.

Problem: The Shift+PrintScreen command prints garbage. See page 99.

Problem: I can't find my fonts, where are they? In the printer? In software? See page 101.

Problem: My file prints oddly. It seems to contain weird characters. See page 103.

Problem: I want to use a font called Benguait, but my application does not offer it. See page 104.

Problem: My application is complaining that it cannot find a font. See page 104.

Problem: My document prints oddly on different computer systems. See page 105.

Chapter 9 Problems with Video Displays

Problem: My manuals talk about all kinds of different display resolutions. I just want to get a monitor that will perform well with my software. What do I look for? See page 109.

Problem: My video card manual brags about being "noninterlaced." Is this a big deal? See page 111.

Problem: What does video memory do? See page 111.

Problem: Should I worry about bus width? See page 112.

Problem: My monitor's connector does not match my computer. See page 112.

Problem: I installed a new video card and it does not work. See page 113.

Problem: I booted my PC but there's no picture on the display. See page 114.

Problem: My video monitor is making a high-pitched whine. See page 114.

Problem: My display is acting like a bad TV set: rolling or showing horizontal bars. See page 115.

Problem: How do I install the software for my new video system? See page 115.

Problem: My computer is giving me an error message like "Bad or missing filename.SYS, Error in CONFIG.SYS line xx." See page 118.

Problem: I installed some new applications software and now my video display does not work correctly. See page 119.

Problem: My screen has "snow" or a funny, colored border around it. See page 120.

Problem: I expected to see a document but I am only seeing garbage. See page 121.

Problem: I expected a different display than I got . . . See page 123.

Chapter 10 Problems with Files

Problem: My computer seems to have lost its personality; it no longer recognizes my commands. It even asked me for the date and time at boot. See page 133.

Problem: My computer is telling me "General failure reading drive A, Abort, Retry, Fail?" See page 137.

Problem: My computer is telling me "File not found - FILENAME.EXT, 0 file(s) copied." See page 138.

Problem: I have misplaced a file somewhere on my disk. See page 138.

Problem: My diskette has been damaged somehow. It no longer contains my files. See page 140.

Problem: I have several copies of a file; which is the latest? See page 142.

Problem: My computer is reporting "Insufficient disk space, 0 File(s) copied." See page 145.

Problem: My application aborted with an "out of memory" error. See page 168.

Problem: My program is running much slower than I expected. See page 170.

Problem: I set up my PC properly, but my program still runs slowly. See page 170.

Problem: I cannot run the same application I used a while ago. See page 172.

Chapter 13 Problems with Software

Problem: I've never installed anything. Where do I begin? See page 179.

Problem: I installed some software, then lost it! See page 181.

Problem: I installed some software, then forgot how to run it. See page 183.

Problem: I installed the software but it won't run properly. See page 184.

Problem: How do I start my new application? See page 187.

Problem: My application worked fine yesterday but it won't run today. See page 188.

Problem: My computer is reporting that it's "out of memory" or has "insufficient memory." See page 189.

Problem: My application program just bombed or returned to DOS unexpectedly. See page 190.

Problem: What's the safest way to upgrade a system? See page 191.

Problem: The upgrade seems incomplete. See page 192.

Problem: My freshly-upgraded system is not working correctly. See page 193.

Problem: The new version of my application won't read older data files. See page 194.

Problem: The new version of my application won't print correctly. See page 195.

Problem: The new version of my application does funny things to my video display. See page 195.

Introduction

Let's get one thing straight right from the beginning: you are a whole lot smarter than a computer. Frankly, computers are dumb—totally, awfully, irreconcilably dumb. Sure, they can add, subtract, multiply, and divide faster than greased lightning—but a housefly is a genius in comparison.

Therefore, if you turn your computer on this morning and it doesn't work properly . . . or if you try to run a program and it bombs . . . or if you just don't get what you thought you should . . . it is not because you aren't smart enough to give the machine the proper instructions. And it (probably) is not because some malevolent spirit has taken residence in that metal box.

Often, it is just because you expect the computer to be smarter than it is. Especially if you are working in DOS or running a new program.

There are times, however, when a switch is in the wrong position, a cable has come loose, or conflicting orders have sent the machine into a midlife crisis. This book is designed to help you find out what the problem is and correct it—as painlessly as possible.

Sure, there may be some new words to learn, but you don't have to learn them all at once. And you certainly don't have to know all of the tech-y words to fix simple problems; you just need to recognize the first signs of trouble and then refer to this book.

Learning to troubleshoot and make simple repairs can be a lot of fun, really. Just follow the directions in the book and pay attention to the safety tips. It also helps to think before you do something that might make your computer look smart—opening up the monitor case and touching the power supply, for instance (plugged in or not, you will gain a new appreciation of the word "shocking").

Purpose and Structure of This Book

The reason for this book is simple: hardware manuals and DOS manuals can be intimidating. There is a need for a book that can talk people through the straightforward task of problem-solving typical personal computer difficulties.

The first chapter of *The PC Answer Book* is devoted to a walk around the system, much as an airline pilot walks around an airplane prior to flying it. The purpose of your walk around is just about the same. You learn about a typical PC setup and about some basic problem-solving skills. In Chapter 2, you take a general look at some typical PC hardware problems that occur during setup.

The middle of the book moves into a symptom/solution format—
a problem is described and the remedies discussed for

- Cables and connectors
- Disks and disk drives
- Keyboards
- Mice and scanners
- Telecommunications
- Printers and fonts
- Video displays
- Files
- Viruses
- DOS and memory
- Application software

This approach allows you to identify your particular problem in the
handy *Help! Table* located at the front of this book and find the page
that helps you solve the situation.

The last chapters and appendix are devoted to information every
computer user has to know. For example, how—and how often—

to back up your data, the proper way to open the computer case to minimize the possibility of damage to you or to the components, and the virtues of keeping a log of changes.

Who Needs This Book?

In the best of all worlds, where computers never develop problems of any nature, this book would be given to a museum to be used as an example of useless writing. Unfortunately, we do not live in the best of all worlds.

If you have a computer and do not enjoy reading thick, technical computer manuals, you need this book.

Conventions Used in This Book

Notes and **Tips** are scattered throughout this book. They are designed to ease your problem-solving.

Cautions present information that will help you keep from hurting yourself physically.

Please follow all safety information. I don't like reading in a hospital bed, do you?

Well, enough beating about the bush, let's get down to it.

Acknowledgments

This book has reached you through the help and encouragement I received from the fine folks at Alpha Books. There are my editors, Susan Klopfer, Nancy Albright, and San Dee Phillips, who helped me find it (again and again). And I want to mention Linda Hawkins, who helped me find it now(!), and Ray Werner, for his wonderful mellowing effect.

I'd also like to thank the rest of Alpha Books' editorial staff, for their devotion to correctness, and the folks in Production, for their devotion to their individual crafts.

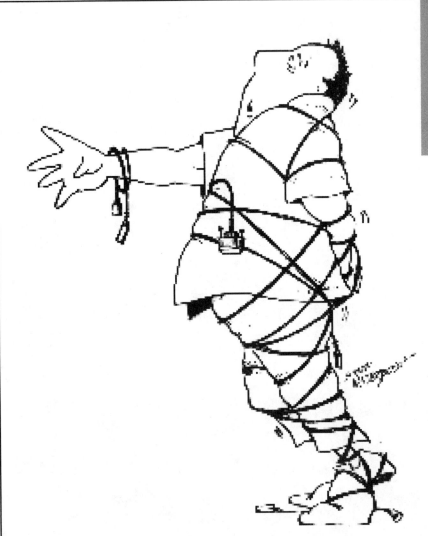

Getting Started

In this chapter you learn personal computer (PC) system basics and names of the various pieces of equipment that typically make up a home personal computer system. Then you move into problem-solving techniques to help you install equipment and identify and solve basic installation-related problems.

The Naming Ritual

Unless you have a very nice computer salesperson, or a son, daughter, friend, or relative who helped you set your computer system up, you discovered on your own that your personal computing system has a monitor, printer, keyboard, the PC itself, maybe a mouse and modem, and perhaps a CD-rom unit.

Your PC—and all its parts—probably look something like Figure 1.1.

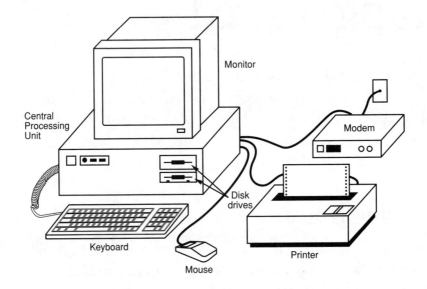

Figure 1.1   Typical computing hardware.

And I know you have cables . . . lots and lots of cables.

Inside the large case, your PC has the actual computer, on a circuit board, a power supply, and one or more disk drives. There is a lot of interesting stuff inside the case, but don't open it until you learn how to do it safely. Static electricity can destroy your computer totally in the blink of an eye.

The Basics of Problem-Solving

Whether you're trying to figure out how to install print drivers or set up a modem, there are some general ways to go about defining and solving problems. These rules range from sharpening your listening skills to simply checking cables when a problem occurs—before taking more drastic measures.

A variety of typical computing problems can be resolved, if you

● Listen to what the computer tries to tell you.

● Keep your manuals handy and refer to them.

● Stay logical.

Listen . . .

Observation is as important with PCs as it is in any other area of life. Unhappy computers often try to tell you what is wrong by producing error messages. Often, these error messages are valuable and useful signposts, like clues to a puzzle. But you must be alert for them. Did the computer report

ERROR #201

or

ERROR #102

Did it tell you

Non-System disk or disk error
Replace and press any key when ready?

or did it complain about a

Bad or missing Command Interpreter?

Or did it just sing you a song of beeps and then freeze up?

If you've spoken with a person just learning English, you know that there are many new and different ways to express an idea. At first you may not understand what is being said, but you refer to dictionaries for definitions and keep trying until communication happens. In the same way, PC error messages can be viewed as a strange dialect, one that needs a specialized dictionary (the user's manual) to understand.

For example, if my computer beeps high-low-low and seems to freeze up, I can look up this symptom in the manual and discover that the keyboard came unplugged.

The moral here is to note the actual text (or sound) of the error message and then refer to an appropriate manual. This pattern-matching works almost every time!

Keep Manuals Handy . . .

Folks seldom read manuals from cover to cover, but they are your first line of defense.

If possible, buy all the manuals you'll need when you purchase the equipment. Everything changes, and new manuals for old computers or software are no longer available as the products mature. You need the ones that came with your gear!

Be Logical . . .

If you think your car is out of gas, do you check the trunk? Probably not. It's only common sense to look at the gas gauge. But PCs don't have gas gauges, so where do you look? Begin by considering the job the computer is supposed to be doing.

For example, if you try to print something and your printer does not respond, consider the flow of information through your system:

1. From the keyboard or mouse

2. To the computer

3. To the printer port

4. To the printer cable

5. To the printer

6. To the paper

In situations like this, it makes sense to start in the middle, in this case, at the cable. If it's OK, then check the far half, the printer:

● Is it plugged in?

● Is it turned on?

● Is it on-line?

● Is it out of paper?

If your cable and printer check out, then check the near half of your system, your computer.

One quick way you can check your computer's ability to print is to exit whatever program you're running and use the DOS PRINT command to print some simple ASCII file. At the C:> prompt, type

print filename>prn

and press **Enter**. Substitute the name of a file in your system for the word **filename** above. Typical choices would be **autoexec.bat** or **config.sys**.

If your printer prints the simple file, your real problem lies with your application program's installation or setup.

In summary, when seeking to solve a problem, take a moment to envision the process and then begin in the middle. Even if you don't find the cause the first time, at least you may be able to eliminate *half* of the possibilities with each new inspection. Just select a new *middle* and try again. This method is called a *binary search* and it is generally much quicker than starting at one end and working your way through to the other end.

This chapter introduced the first three troubleshooting rules: listen to what the computer tries to tell you, keep your manuals handy and refer to them, and be logical.

Now let's move on to Chapter 2 and continue with general trouble-shooting ideas about cables and connectors, disks and disk drives, switches, keyboards, and other parts of your PC system.

chapter **2**

General Troubleshooting

In this chapter, you take a quick walk through your personal computer system and talk about some general hardware troubleshooting activities. You start with cables and connectors, then move through disks and disk drives, and on to keyboards. Input and output devices are discussed, including mice, scanners, modems, printers, and video systems.

Before we continue, however, here's a story of a friend's embarrassing moment. Remember, computers aren't too swift. But the person running the computer isn't always plugged in, either.

A friend had just finished a long and involved article for publication, and had stored it on a floppy disk to send to the publisher. He decided to make a few minor changes, plopped the disk back into the machine, and called up the file. The machine spoke:

Error reading drive A:

The blood drained from his face. A good fifteen hours of work on that disk and he had been so smug that he hadn't even backed it up! Gone! The deadline was the next morning. He cried.

Reaching down to tear the offending disk out of the computer, he noticed that something didn't look quite right. He opened the door, and the disk popped out, sideways. Golly . . .

Add two more general troubleshooting rules to your list as we address topics in this chapter:

● Don't assume the worst case until you have eliminated any people errors.

● If it was working yesterday but does not work today, ask yourself, "What changed?"

Cables and Connectors

> **CAUTION**
>
> *Always turn off your system and unplug it before handling, installing, or removing any electrical cables.*

Many parts of a computer system are connected by low-voltage electrical cables called *data cables*. These cables are usually named for the device they connect to the PC, so the most common ones are

● Keyboard cables

● Video cables

● Printer cables

● Modem cables

Cables that are located inside the case generally work fine unless the PC is repaired, shipped, or jarred harshly. External cables can, and do, cause problems, particularly at the connectors, because they are subject to strain and abuse.

If you suspect a problem with your equipment, and check the cables and connectors, you may find that they are loose or frayed. Frayed cables can be a safety hazard as well as a nuisance, so they need to be replaced.

Peripherals are items not central to a system, but added around the outside instead. Many peripherals, such as keyboards and printers, are connected to your computer by data cables. Cables generally can be connected only to the type of peripheral (printer, modem, etc.) for which they are designed, because the connectors on the ends are different. You may have problems if your PC has several of the same type of connectors, because a cable can be properly hooked up in the wrong place. If this is a problem, don't be afraid to label the cables. This is why engineers use blueprints and why drivers refer to maps in unfamiliar territory.

Get in the habit of always fastening cables securely. Most cable connectors include small screws to secure them to both the computer and the peripheral—use them. Yes, they are more trouble to remove but also less prone to come loose or fall off. Loose cables are almost worse than no cable because the electrical connection may become unreliable.

Compare the construction of the data cables you buy and avoid flimsy cables or connectors.

The most common data cable connectors have industrial-strength names such as DB-25 and DB-15. DB indicates a style of connector and the number tells how many pins it can have. Table 2.1 lists the common connectors found on most PCs and their purposes. Notice that these connectors generally have gender, so your cable must be the correct gender to fit the *port*, or socket, on the computer.

Table 2.1   Common Cable Connectors.

Connector	*Purpose*
Round din	Keyboard or mouse
DB-9 female	Monochrome, CGA, EGA video port
DB-9 male	AT-style serial port for modems and mice
DB-15 female	Game port
DB-16 female	VGA video port
DB-25 female	Parallel printer port
DB-25 male	Serial port for modems and mice

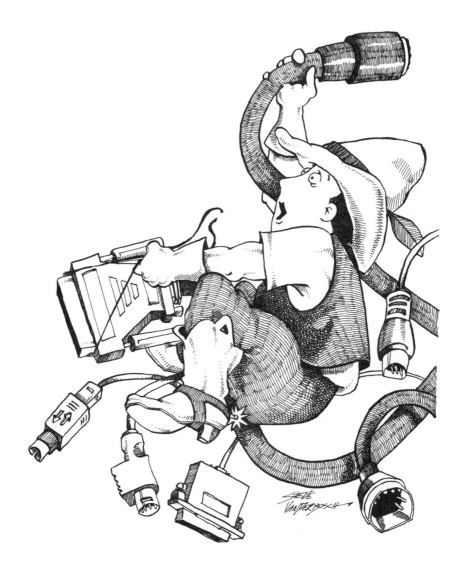

See Chapter 3, "Problems with Cables and Connectors," for more information.

Disks and Disk Drives

We've all seen tape recorders and cassette recorders. In these machines, a magnetic tape is pulled past a special head which records or plays the music on the tape. *Disk drives* work the same way except that the tape is a spinning disk and the head moves in and out across the surface of the disk to locate the data. Disk drives play data instead of music.

Disk drives are available in two flavors: *fixed* and *floppy*. The big difference is that *floppy diskettes* can be removed from the drive mechanism, and *fixed disks* generally cannot. Although we speak of *internal* and *external drives*, most of them are actually installed inside the PC chassis and the term "internal" has come to be synonymous with "fixed."

Most PCs have one or more disk drives, either totally enclosed inside the case or with a slot that allows you to insert floppy diskettes. This book does not explain how to install or replace disk drives, but we can tell you about some common problems and give you some tips on avoiding disaster.

The big difference between fixed drives and floppy drives is that floppy diskettes can be removed from the drive and fixed disks cannot.

As PCs have matured, manufacturers keep finding ways to stuff more data onto floppy diskettes. A few years ago, diskettes could store only 360 kilobytes (360K). A *byte* is one character of information, and a 360K diskette stored a book of about 400 pages. Now they easily can store 1.2M (1.2 megabytes, over a million bytes) or more—a book of 1,500 pages or so.

See Chapter 4, "Problems with Disks and Disk Drives," for more information about floppy and hard drives.

The Keyboard

TIP

If you are sneakernetting (a tech-y term for moving data between your work and home PCs by walking disks back and forth), use diskettes with a capacity acceptable to all the machines.

As PCs have evolved, their keyboards have matured from the older AT-style (with just over 80 keys) to the modern enhanced style (with over 100 keys in a different, wider layout). This can be important because older keyboards may not work with modern PCs. Some keyboards have a switch on the bottom to accommodate either type of system (AT-style or enhanced), but most have no switch and function only with the appropriate PC.

Keyboards normally are not serviceable; they either work or they do not. PC keyboards contain a small, local computer to observe your finger on a key and send the correct scan code to the larger computer.

The only things you need to know about keyboards are

- They are available in a variety of styles.
- They may have an AT/XT switch on the bottom.
- Their *LEDs* (light-emitting diodes or little green lights) should flash when the computer boots.
- Prolonged strain can damage their connectors, at the computer.
- Spilling liquids on them can damage them.

See Chapter 5, "Problems with Keyboards," for more information.

The Mouse

A mouse is a simple input device, consisting of a roller and a couple of buttons, but it takes its directions from special software called a *driver* that is included with the mouse when you purchase it.

If your mouse is not functioning, here are some things you can do right away:

- Check to see if your mouse is connected to the proper port on the back of your PC.
- Reboot your PC and watch the screen carefully. Look for a message indicating that the mouse was "found" and which serial port it was found on (COM1, COM2, etc.).

● Ensure that the software you're using is set to expect the mouse on the same port.

A mouse and an external modem both occupy a serial port in your PC. They must occupy different ports. If you install both devices on one port, they conflict, with unpredictable results. Mice and other input devices generally come with diagnostic programs to help you troubleshoot such problems.

In general, if you are installing a mouse for the first time, do it very carefully. See Chapter 6, "Problems with Mice and Scanners," for more information.

The Modem

More home and small-business computer users are adding *modems* to their systems because they connect with service bureaus and bulletin boards. A modem converts computer signals to and from a form that telephone lines can transmit. The name, a contraction of MOdulate/ DEModulate, was coined long before the PC industry existed. A modem may be installed inside your PC or you may have an external unit. In either case, it occupies one of your serial ports (COM1, COM2, etc.) and can conflict with other serial devices, such as a mouse, if installed improperly.

If your external modem is not functioning properly, the first thing you can do is check to see that its cables are properly connected and in good repair. Are you using a real modem cable? Other cables can appear to be the same but actually can be wired differently.

Modems are used with special programs called *telecommunication software* or *terminal emulators*. These programs run on your PC and use a serial port to control the modem, to send and receive data over your telephone line.

Today's modems are very fast and priced reasonably. External modems usually have several switches that are sold preset to the most common configuration. I've seldom ever needed to change them, nor will you.

When you purchase a modem, it's a good idea to compare its original jumper and switch settings with the manual to establish the basic setup. You then should record any setup changes you make in the manual, or in a logbook. Proper attention to this can save hours of frustration.

To get a modem running correctly, you must

- Connect it to a working telephone line.
- Connect it to a serial port (if it's an external model).

- Set a switch or jumper on the modem to determine which serial port it will use (if it's an internal unit).

- Set up your telecommunications software the same way.

For more information about setting up modems and their software, see Chapter 7, "Telecommunications and Problems with Ports."

Printers

Printers are like some cars—they work fine until you really need them. Fortunately, printers are easier and cheaper to fix. Most printer problems can be grouped into one of two categories: troubles at the printer or troubles with the software that's driving it.

Early printers had many switches to determine their setup. Newer printers still have switches but they also can be controlled with software, from the PC. This is good if you like remote control but bad if you like doing things in one certain way. Switches, and how to reset them, are further discussed in Chapter 8, "Problems with Printers and Fonts."

TIP

Your printer was sold with preset configurations. Check your manual to locate any switches and establish their default settings. You may be able to reset the printer to its factory default settings.

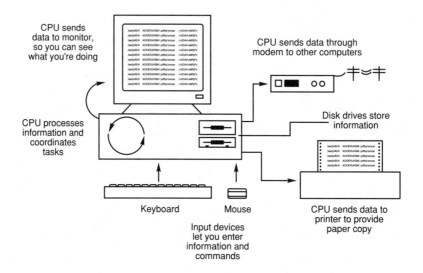

CPU sends data to monitor, so you can see what you're doing

CPU sends data through modem to other computers

CPU processes information and coordinates tasks

Disk drives store information

Keyboard

Mouse

CPU sends data to printer to provide paper copy

Input devices let you enter information and commands

Figure 2.1 How a computer system works.

Your printer probably has a built-in self-test mode, usually accessed by pressing a special combination of buttons while turning it on. Read your printer's manual to learn how to perform this test. If the printer passes it, your problem is somewhere before the printer in the flow of data.

Of course, your printer may just be *off-line.* If it has a button or key on its front panel for this, it must be *on-line* to respond to your computer. Usually, the same button reverses the condition. When a printer is off-line, it's not listening to your computer at all. Look for a light on the printer that indicates this status.

Whenever you're having a printer problem, the first thing to do is stop and ask: Is my printer plugged in? Turned on? On-line? Check the cables, too.

See Chapter 8, "Problems with Printers and Fonts," for more specific information on troubleshooting printer problems.

Video Systems

Your car has a dashboard and so does your computer. A PC's dashboard is its keyboard and video monitor—together. Actually, the monitor (similar to your television set) is only half of the video system; the other half is a circuit board inside the PC.

Video monitors work the same way your television set does: they form a picture from very small dots of light. Each dot is a *pixel* (picture element), and video monitors are rated in quality by how many dots they can produce, called the *resolution*. More dots cost more money and give better resolution.

In the last few years, video systems have evolved from MGA (monochrome) to CGA (color), then to EGA, VGA, Super VGA, and now XGA. These names are all contractions indicating the amount of *resolution* they have and how many colors they can display—the more colors offered, the higher the cost. The *GA* stands for Graphics Adapter in all but VGA systems, where it means Graphics Array. I've listed them here in the order they appeared, which is also an indication of their price.

For best results, video cards (the circuit board in the PC) must match the monitor with which they're used. These cards also contain various amounts of video memory, and more is better. The present standard is 1M for VGA systems. This on-board video memory speeds up the entire system by freeing the PC to do other things besides updating the display.

If you are installing a video system in a PC, read the manuals closely. Incorrect switch or jumper settings can damage some of the newer monitors. Don't change the switches on a video card unless you know what you're doing; the results can be expensive. Look for keywords such as "multiple-frequency" and "band-width."

Problems usually arise only if the system is allowed to gather dust (monitors generate huge amounts of static electricity). And of course, the cables must be kept well connected and in good repair.

CAUTION

Inspect the back of your monitor occasionally. If you notice lots of dust, have the monitor cleaned by a technician. Don't attempt to open the monitor by yourself!

Video boards are sold with a variety of special driver programs, tailored to certain popular applications such as Lotus 1-2-3 and Windows. Your video system generally functions properly with no special driver installed. At boot, the PC "finds" the video card and passes temporary control to it. It sets up the situation it requires, then gives control back to the PC, which continues with the boot process.

It's a good idea to watch your computer as it boots. Because error messages must be displayed on the screen, one of the first things the PC does is to let the video system install itself. The early messages you see during boot concern the video card.

See Chapter 9, "Problems with Video Displays," for more specific information.

When you become a seasoned PC user, you find that solving computer programs gets a little easier. You learn that it pays not to overreact when a problem occurs. The problem, after all, might be a loose cable, or caused by changes made by someone else.

The next chapter begins a new section of this book. Each chapter presents typical problems or questions followed by detailed answers, often accompanied by stepped-out instructions.

Problems with Cables and Connectors

PCs are like octopi. They have tentacles that seem to go everywhere . . . to keyboards, mice, video monitors, printers, modems, telephones, and even some hard drives. Unfortunately, these tentacles have a lot in common with a salamander's tail — they have a tendency to come loose. And, unlike that tail, cables tend to stay just enough in their proper place to make problem-solving difficult. Happily, the great majority of problems that pop up with devices that are attached to the computer can be solved with a deftly applied wiggle or a gentle poke. Because we often encounter connector problems when installing new equipment, this chapter also includes some installation hints and thoughts about compatibility.

Problem: I turned my computer on, but nothing happens.

Solution: Is it plugged in? On both ends? Is there power to that wall socket?

Sure, you can laugh, but this has happened to me and many other folks. Try plugging a lamp into the wall socket; if it lights, the problem is not with the power. If it doesn't, look to see if a circuit breaker has blown or a ground fault indicator has popped. If all else fails, call an electrician.

If you have power to the wall socket, check to see if the computer's power cord is bad. The best way to do this is to borrow one from a friend and try it on your machine.

If your computer is still dead, it's time for a trip to the repair shop.

Problem: My computer cannot "find" my keyboard at boot.

Solution: Keyboards and mice get more wear than other peripherals because they are also connected to us! It may need replacing.

If you get this message:

Keyboard Error, Press F2 To Continue

check the cable to see if it's properly plugged in. Give it a gentle but firm wiggle. (This message should make all of us feel quite superior to that computer. Really, if the computer can't find its keyboard, how in the heck is it going to know that you pressed F2?)

If this doesn't correct the problem, borrow a friend's keyboard, or try yours on his or her system. Keyboards are seldom worth fixing, and the best course of action — if it is really broken — is to replace it.

Problem: I just turned on my computer and my mouse isn't working.

Solution: Is it still connected to your computer? Is the wire damaged near the connector?

Mice are often dropped, or moved from computer to computer, so their connectors get loosened and broken more frequently than many other peripherals.

If the problem persists, see Chapter 6, "Problems with Mice and Scanners," for more information.

Problem: My printer is turned on, and its lights are lit, but when I try to print a file, nothing happens, or I get an error message that says something like

> **Errors on list device indicate that it may be off-line.**
> **Please check it.**

Solution: Your printer cable may have come loose, or your printer may be off-line.

Be sure to check both ends of the cable and then look for a light on the printer's control panel that shows if it is on-line or off-line. Do you have more than one printer? Are you using a switch box to share one printer port? You may need to flip a switch to actually connect your printer to your computer.

Printer problems can also be caused by software. See Chapter 8, "Problems with Printers and Fonts," for a discussion of other problem sources.

Problem: My old cable does not fit my new printer.

Solution: Recall that printers are available with several types of interfaces: serial, parallel, and even Centronics. You need the correct cable and, perhaps, the correct card inside your printer.

Some printers come with the appropriate cables. Contact the salespeople where you purchased the printer.

Problem: I tried to attach my new gee-whiz video monitor to my computer and found that the connectors don't match.

Solution: Inexpensive adapters are available to convert most video monitors to most video cards. The most common one converts 9-pin EGA cables to 15-pin VGA connectors.

Go laugh at the guy who sold you the monitor; he missed an opportunity to sell you an expensive new video card, too. Now he gets to sell only a cheap adapter. Actually, video systems have improved as they have evolved.

Because the manufacturers want to appeal to the most customers, they generally make their monitors backward-compatible. This means that your new monitor can work with your old video card. There are some exceptions, however, so check with your dealer. In general, a new monitor is of little use without a new, better video card.

Problem: My external modem is not working correctly.

Solution #1: Is it turned on?

Because it's an external modem, you generally should see some activity— some lights lit when it's on—even if your PC is off.

Solution #2: Are all the wire connections intact?

Modems have more wires than any other peripheral. They connect to your PC and the telephone lines and sometimes the AC power line.

Solution #3: Are you using the correct cable between the modem and the telephone jack in the wall?

Telephones use a funny, fragile little "RJ-11-style" connector. Because modems must connect to the telephone line, they use the same connector. Notice that your telephone uses a similar, but different, connector between the instrument and the handset. Look closely and you'll see that the two connectors have different numbers of contacts, so they cannot be used interchangeably.

Solution #4: Are you using the correct cable between the modem and your PC?

Unfortunately, all modem cables are not created equal. Some extension cables for printers look exactly like modem cables—but they're wired differently. Be sure you're using the correct cable!

Problem: My internal modem is not working correctly.

Solution #1: Are you using the correct cable between the modem and the telephone jack in the wall?

See the discussion of these cables in the previous problem/solution.

Solution #2: How do you know it's not working correctly? Have you queried the modem?

All Hayes-compatible modems (internal or external) should respond to a special query. Try typing **at** and pressing Enter from within your telecommunications program. If your modem answers **OK**, you know it's listening and talking to your PC correctly.

If you don't get the **OK** response, see if your telecommunications software is configured for the same serial port (COM1, for example) as your modem. It's usually easier to change your software configuration than to open up the PC and change a jumper or switch on the modem board, but that also is a possibility. Your software and your modem must both be set to use the same communication port. And no other device (a mouse, perhaps?) can be using that serial port!

Problem: My computer has a SCSI PORT but it does not recognize some or all of the devices connected to the port.

Solution #1: Did you just connect yet another device to your SCSI network?

SCSI (pronounced "skuzzy") stands for Small Computer System Interface. SCSI ports are a good example of peripherals that send high-speed signals through short cables. You must rethink the terminations along the whole cable whenever you connect another device, and there is a limit to the number of devices you can connect to one network. See the manuals that came with your new device for more information about terminations.

Solution #2: Each SCSI device must have a unique address (identifier) on the network.

The address is usually established by a switch on the device. Your new device may be conflicting with an existing one, or loading (shorting out) the whole SCSI network. Try disconnecting the device and rebooting.

Problem: My computer cannot find its external hard disk. It won't boot properly.

Solution: Is the disk properly connected? Turned on? These cables are usually short because they must carry high-speed signals.

This chapter shows you that the octopus' arms can be your friend or a pretty crafty foe. Generally, a little attention, a wiggle, or a poke will solve quite a few problems. Now let's move on to disks and drives.

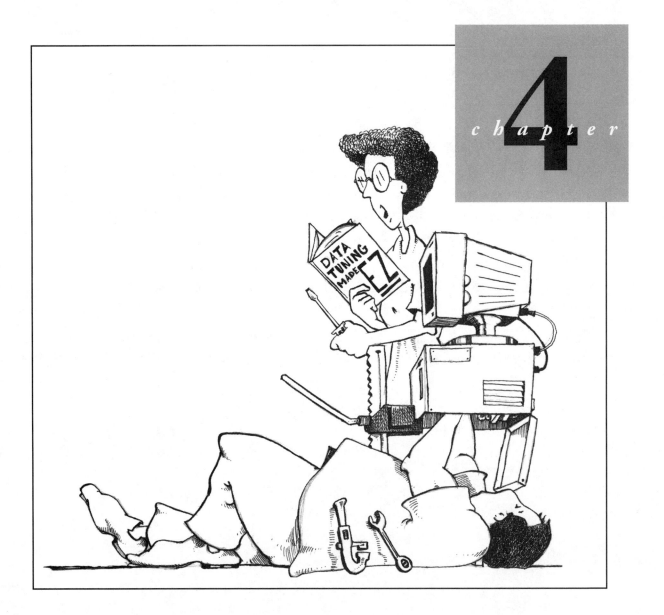

Problems with Disks and Disk Drives

Most PCs have one or more disk drives. Recall that disk drives are available in two flavors: fixed and floppy. The big difference is that floppy diskettes can be removed from the drive and fixed disks cannot.

As PCs have matured, manufacturers have created systems that can store even more and more information. A few years ago, diskettes could store only 360K (kilobytes); now they can store 1.2M (megabytes) or more per diskette. You need to know the maximum capacity of each floppy disk drive in your system because it cannot read or write diskettes of greater capacity. This can cause problems if you wish to move data among machines on diskettes. See Figure 4.1.

Hard drives communicate with the computer via an electrical interface. These interfaces have names like MFM, IDE, and SCSI. Some of them can move data more swiftly than others. The fastest ones, SCSI interfaces, are also the most expensive. IDE interfaces are just a bit slower and much cheaper. MFM interfaces are the slowest and are falling out of fashion.

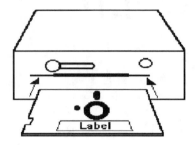

Figure 4.1 Be sure to insert the disk properly into its drive.

Problem: My PC won't read my diskette. It's giving me a message that says

Invalid media

Solution: Your diskette may be formatted to the wrong density for your diskette drive.

Diskettes can be formatted to several different data densities. For example, large 5¼-inch diskettes can be formatted to hold 360K or 1.2M of data, depending upon the quality (cost) of the diskette (see Figure 4.2). Three and one-half inch diskettes can be formatted to contain 360K, 720K, or 1.44M of data.

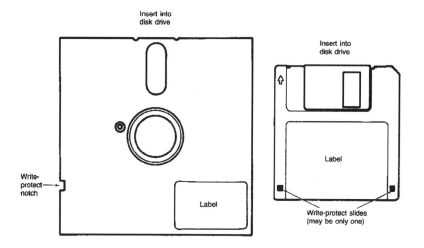

Figure 4.2 The two sizes of floppy disks.

You can recognize 1.44M diskettes because they have two holes along the top, but the only reliable way to tell if a large diskette should be formatted to 1.2M is to look on the package. Simply trying to format a large diskette to 1.2M is a bad idea because it may work this time but then fail later, unless the manufacturer has guaranteed the quality.

If you put a 1.2M diskette in a drive that can read only 360K densities, it thinks the diskette is unformatted because it cannot read it.

One way to tell what drive you have is to format a blank diskette. Be sure to use the best diskette available—one that can be formatted to

1.2M or 1.44M. The drive usually defaults to the highest possible density.

If you notice that the drive is taking a long time to format the diskette, or making lots of grinding sounds, you may be using an inferior diskette.

Problem: My PC won't boot. My screen tells me

> **Non-System disk or disk error**
> **Replace and press any key when ready**

or

> **Bad or missing Command Interpreter**

Solution #1: If the little latch on your floppy drive is closed but there's no diskette in the drive, flip the latch open so the machine can ignore the A: drive and boot to your hard disk.

This probably is the most common error message you'll ever see. At boot, most PCs check for a bootable system diskette in the A: drive before seeking the same thing on an internal, fixed disk. If the A: drive contains a system diskette, the computer boots to it. If the drive has no diskette, or if the door latch is open, the computer continues on, to inspect the fixed disk.

Solution #2: The diskette in your A: drive is not bootable.

Use a bootable diskette. See the FORMAT command in your DOS manual.

Solution #3: The diskette in your A: drive may be installed sideways or upside down.

Ensure that it's correctly placed in the drive. (Hey, it happens.)

Solution #4: Your hard drive is not (or is no longer) bootable.

This is one of the more serious problems you may encounter, but it's not the end of the world! If your hard drive was bootable previously, its COMMAND.COM file may have been modified or erased accidentally. If your hard drive was not bootable to begin with, you need to review how you've been booting your computer until now.

Here's a simple test: First, put a bootable diskette in your A: drive, then reboot the computer by pressing the Ctrl, Alt, and Del keys simultaneously and releasing them. When your computer has finished booting, and you have the A:> DOS prompt, type **dirc:**, then press **Enter**. The root directory of the C: drive will be listed on the screen. You cannot do any damage with this command, but you can learn a lot about your data and your hard drive's health!

If you find your files anywhere on the C: drive, use the DOS COPY command to copy a few files to diskettes immediately, then take them to another machine and establish that you really have recovered them intact. Do not attempt to format diskettes on your machine; use the other computer, for simplicity and data safety. The general format for the COPY command to use in this case is

copy source\destination

or, for example,

copy c:\files\myfile.doc a:

Notice that you need to specify the complete, exact source file-name, but you do not have to repeat it for the destination, unless you wish to rename the file at the same time. In the example, the file MYFILE.DOC is copied to the current directory of the diskette in the A: drive as MYFILE.DOC.

When you have saved what you can, contact your PC repairman, or the shop where you bought the computer, and discuss the problem. You may need to replace or reformat your hard drive, which should not be attempted until you are sure you've obtained whatever data remains intact!

If the data on your hard drive is important, there are several disk maintenance and repair programs that may be able to recover some or all of it. You could contact your local university or PC club and appeal for helpful advice. Often, there are knowledgeable local folks who will help you just for the fun of it.

If the data on your hard drive is extremely important, you may be able to return the hard drive to the factory, or hire a local computer jockey to recover it, even if the personnel at the computer store claim it's lost permanently. Such a recovery effort undoubtedly will cost a lot of money and take at least several days.

Unfortunately, these errors do occur occasionally, and most folks learn to back up their data regularly. You're much better off if you learn that lesson the easy way—by following this advice!

Problem: It seems to take a long time to read and write files to my hard drive. My machine used to do that much faster.

Solution: Your hard drive may need to be *defragmented.*

When DOS stores a file, it puts as much as it can in the next available place on your hard drive. Eventually, your files may become scattered all over your disk, in tiny pieces. You may notice that it takes your PC a loooooooong time to read or write even a relatively small file.

The way to avoid this is to defragment your hard drive occasionally. To do this, you run a special program that collects your files together into sensible groups. Ask for a defragmenter at your local software store.

Problem: My PC reports

Sector not found

when it tries to read a floppy diskette.

Solution #1: Your diskette may have been damaged by magnetism or spilled coffee.

Try to read the diskette on another machine—preferably the one that formatted the diskette—before concluding that the data is lost.

Solution #2: Your disk drive may need a tune-up.

Diskette drives are supposed to rotate the diskette at a certain speed. And it would be a nicer world if they all rotated the same, but the mechanical nature of these critters means that sooner or later they speed up or slow down.

Diskette drives should be checked for proper speed at least once each year. You can buy a utility to do this or you can have it checked when you send the system out for its annual cleaning. Yes, an annual cleaning is a very good idea! Read on.

Problem: I put my diskette in a friend's machine and got the dread sector-not-found error message.

Solution: Don't panic! This may mean only that one of the machine's diskette drives is running at a different speed than the other drive.

Try the diskette in another machine, and in the original drive, before concluding that you've lost the data.

If you get a sector-not-found error message when the PC attempts to read any diskette, don't despair; the data is probably not lost, but that particular drive just cannot find it. Try to read the diskette on another disk drive, perhaps on another machine. Or go back and try to read the diskette in the original drive. One of the machine's drives may just need a tune-up or speed adjustment.

Problem: My PC occasionally gives the sector-not-found message when reading my hard drive, but then it finds other files easily.

Solution: Your hard drive's data may need a tune-up.

Can you tune up data? Not really, but you can fine-tune its location on your disk. Hard drives normally are not serviced in the field. They must be returned for "depot level" maintenance, so folks generally conclude that they do not need routine service . . . but this is not necessarily so.

Hard drives are subject to mechanical wear, which eventually causes the read/write heads to miss the place on the disk where it stored your data, producing the error message. This devastating experience usually can be avoided by a special type of tune-up. Several popular programs, Spinrite, for instance, can examine your drive and subtly alter the location of the data, to center it beneath the moving head.

Avoid these problems by tuning up your data with one of these special programs every few months. They do not retrieve lost data but they definitely help you retain the data you have.

Problem: I ran CHKDSK and it reports lost chains or clusters.

Solution #1: One of the programs you are using is a shoddy housekeeper.

Use CHKDSK (Check Disk) frequently until you can identify which program is the offender, then complain to the software company that wrote the program. You may receive a free upgrade!

Some programs are better housekeepers than others. If a program bombs or the power is lost, they do not finish writing data to a disk. If this continues, the disk eventually fills up with junk data that is unused but occupies space on your disk. The creators of DOS realized that this might happen and provided the CHKDSK program.

Solution #2: You may need a UPS (uninterruptible power supply) if you live in a neighborhood with "dirty" electrical power.

Be sure to read the DOS manual carefully before you use CHKDSK, and use it only occasionally. Use it to scan your hard drive, repair broken data chains, and move data from bad areas to safer ones.

Alternatively, if your AC power is interrupted momentarily, your computer can alter or lose small amounts of data during the interruption. This occurs when the electrical signals are jangled. If this happens to you frequently, consider buying a UPS to smooth out the power to your computer.

Problem: The diskettes in my disk drive become hot during use.

Solution: Your fan may be broken!

Unlike the solid-state components in your PC, disk drives are mechanical contraptions, subject to wear and tear. They are also subject to heat damage because they are located inside your PC, among lots of circuits that generate heat.

Most computers (except laptops and notebooks) have a fan to cool the power supply. The fan usually is located at the rear of the machine. Check the fan occasionally to be sure it's actually running. A dead fan can kill an expensive power supply or fixed disk!

We all know that dirt is a machine's worst enemy. How clean is your computer? That fan can suck in a lot of small grit and fluff which can cause random electrical errors and even cause a major short-circuit eventually. Many local companies now offer computer cleaning services. For a nominal fee they disassemble your PC and remove accumulations of dust and other material that may degrade your machine's cooling ability or cause electrical problems.

Inspect the fan on the rear of your computer. If the grill is clogged with dust, consider what the inside of the machine must be like and then get your PC cleaned promptly! And have the diskette drives tuned up at the same time. A small fee now will save large bills and lost data later!

This is one of the more difficult chapters because we introduce some new terminology and deal with the concept of losing your data! You learn a lot about disks, sizes, and formats, and you see that housekeeping is important. Well, you made it, and you know that your data isn't usually really lost, after all! Now let's look at some of the ways your keyboard could plague you. After this chapter, the next one is a snap!

R.I.P.

This keyboard wasn't working,
And we did all the manual said,
But the problems were still lurking,
So we figured it must be dead!

Problems with Keyboards

Ah, keyboards . . . our whip to tame the beast. The dashboard. Fun, when they work right. But occasionally they don't. Fortunately, there's not much that can go wrong with a keyboard. Keyboards are the main member in a group of peripherals called input devices for obvious reasons.

Problem: EVERYTHING I TYPE IS IN CAPITAL LETTERS! HOW CAN I GET BACK TO lowercase letters?

Solution: Your CapsLock key is on. (And the associated LED should also be lit.) Press CapsLock once. Now you should get lowercase letters—unless you press the Shift key, of course.

Notice that computer keyboards do another funny thing, differently than a real typewriter. The CapsLock key actually inverts the Shift key's operation. If CapsLock is on, pressing Shift and typing produces lowercase letters. The CapsLock key is a toggle.

Problem: My arrow keys make numbers on my screen instead of moving the cursor.

Solution: Your NumLock key is on. See if the LED is lit. Press the key once to turn it off, once again to turn it back on. This key also is a toggle.

Problem: What's the ScrollLock key for?

Solution: I never have figured that out. I just ignore it. It's never bothered me.

Problem: My keyboard is dead.

Solution: Is it plugged in? We tug and haul and wiggle on these cords. Is yours broken? Have you stretched it too far in an attempt to get comfortable?

If the cord is twisted near the connector, or bent at a sharp angle, wiggle it and see if the keyboard regains its sanity. If so, you need a new cord. It's a cheap problem to fix. If not, read on.

Problem: My keyboard is still dead.

Solution: Reboot your computer. Most keyboards have at least three LEDs to show the position of the CapsLock, NumLock, and ScrollLock keys (see Figure 5.1).

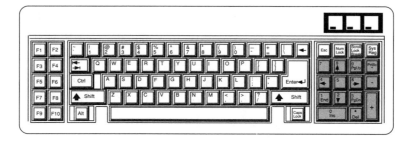

Figure 5.1 A computer keyboard.

If you have these keys, they probably flash at boot, when the computer welcomes the keyboard to the party. Reboot your box now, and see if the LEDs flash as they should. If not, you may get an error message such as

Invalid keyboard

or

Keyboard not found

If possible, try another keyboard. Yours may have an internal problem.

Problem: I tried another keyboard, which also didn't work.

Solution: Are you certain it was the correct type of keyboard?

If your PC beeped and said

Interface/Keyboard error

or something similar, you may have tried the wrong kind of keyboard. You need to know that there are two types: those for the old 8086 and 8088 machines—confusingly called IBM PCs—and those for 286 and higher machines. Many keyboards have a switch on the underside, to select the keyboard type. Keyboards aren't cheap, but they're not nearly as expensive as computers, either.

Generally, you won't do permanent damage by using the wrong switch setting, so go ahead and experiment!

Problem: My keyboard makes garbage. I press one key and the wrong character appears on my screen.

Solution: Assuming that no one's playing a trick on you by changing your system's COUNTRY or KEYB specifications, your keyboard is probably broken.

So, what are COUNTRY and KEYB specifications? Recent versions of DOS let you customize your system to your culture. You can use these commands to select foreign character sets, keyboard layouts, and punctuation conventions. However, these changes require alterations to your CONFIG.SYS file, which do not usually happen accidentally. See Chapter 10, "Problems with Files," (the first problem) for help with altering a CONFIG.SYS file.

Meanwhile, try turning your entire system off for perhaps ten minutes, then reboot. If the problem recurs, call your dealer.

Problem: My new keyboard has the keys in different, irritating places.

Solution: Some keyboards let you choose where certain keys are located.

With these keyboards, you can flip a switch on the bottom of the keyboard to swap or remap the keys (usually only the Ctrl and CapsLock keys). Look for a switch and read the literature that came with your PC for more information.

Problem: What's an *enhanced keyboard?*

Solution: When PCs were first introduced, their keyboards had the *function keys* located on the left side and the arrow (cursor) keys embedded in the numeric keypad. These early keyboards included only ten function keys (F1, F2, etc.).

Eventually, manufacturers offered longer, enhanced keyboards with twelve function keys and a duplicate set of editing and arrow keys in the middle. In most cases, the numeric keypad and editing keys also are available in the numeric keypad, to suit user preferences.

Problem: My keyboard is really dead.

Solution: Was it disconnected recently?

If you accidentally disconnect your keyboard, be sure to turn the PC off, then reconnect it and turn the PC back on. Your computer needs to "see" the keyboard at boot. It cannot find it if you connect it (or reconnect it) later.

Problem: My CapsLock key is up but the LED says it's down.

Solution: The LEDs on your keyboard should always show the present position of your NumLock, CapsLock, and ScrollLock keys.

If you notice that the LEDs remain illuminated even when the keys are unlocked (that is, up), your keyboard, cable, or connector may be defective, or your PC may have booted improperly for some other reason. Reboot the PC and watch the video monitor carefully for error messages or other signs of trouble.

TIP

The LEDs on your keyboard should always indicate the positions of their respective keys. If they do otherwise, try rebooting your computer.

Now you know that there aren't many things that you can do to your keyboard, or ways that it can go bad. And it's pretty easy to tell if it's not working correctly. Did you notice that we didn't discuss software drivers for this peripheral? That's because the keyboard driver software is built right into your PC and it's a pretty standard item. Keyboards really are quite foolproof, unlike our next topic: mice.

Problems with Mice and Scanners

Have you ever watched people drive? Some are hesitant, some deliberate, and others seem to attack the road as if it were a mortal enemy.

Recently, as I watched some people play with various mice at a local computer shop, I realized that some of the same principles apply. After all, mice, trackballs, and steering wheels are all input devices—they put information into your PC. See Figure 6.1. Scanners are input devices, too, although they do a more complex job than a mouse. Fortunately for our problem-solving purposes, most of the time we fix mice and trackball problems the same way we fix scanners—because they use serial ports and require software.

In this chapter, we'll take a look at how these input devices connect you to your computer and consider some things that can disconnect them at the wrong time. Although we talk, for the most part, about mice, the same information applies to trackballs and other pointing devices.

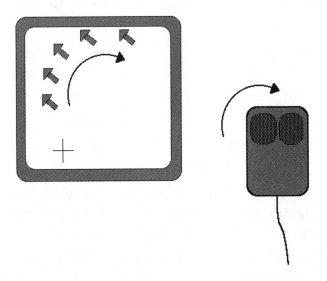

Fig. 6.1   Control your screen with a mouse.

Problem: My mouse came with both a *com* file and a *sys* file. What are they? Which one should I use?

Solution: Use either one, but not both, and know that they install differently. These programs are "drivers" your computer needs in order to listen to your mouse.

The com files (such as mouse.com) are *memory-resident* programs that you can install by typing their name at the DOS prompt. You can do this at any time, but you only need to do it once after your computer boots. This is the simplest method, and many folks add a line to their AUTOEXEC.BAT file so that their mouse is installed automatically each time they turn on their computer. The com version is probably the best general choice.

The sys files (mouse.sys, for example) are device drivers, meant to be installed from your CONFIG.SYS file when your computer boots. They do the same thing as the com files, but they get installed earlier in your computer's boot process.

Problem: My mouse (scanner) is not working.

Solution #1: It may need AC power.

Some peripherals require an extra power supply that plugs into the wall, as well as the cable that connects to your computer. If the power supply is unplugged, your mouse (or scanner) is dead. Check your cabling. Check the wall socket by plugging a lamp into it. Look for a light on the device that indicates that it's receiving AC power.

Solution #2: It may need to be reset.

Some peripherals contain a small, local computer (or microprocessor) to give them the "intelligence" to do their job. For best results, you really should boot all your peripherals first, then turn on your computer.

If you are using a plug strip and are having occasional, odd problems with your system, try turning things on in the above sequence, instead of all at once with the plug strip switch. If you detect a pattern, consult your retailer or the person responsible for your system.

Because the plug strips may also contain *surge protectors* which can be beneficial to your system, consider forming the habit of turning your system on in the correct sequence: First the peripherals, then the actual computer.

Solution #3: You may need to change your device's software setup.

Scanners and other serial devices are usually connected to serial ports on the back of your PC. Because you may have several serial ports, the application software that came with the scanner, serial mouse or other peripheral, may have a setup program or menu to configure it, or tell it which port has the hardware!

Solution #4: You may need to install, or reinstall, your device's driver software.

Mouse software? Yup. Like many other PC accessories, mice need a driver program. Not all mice come with drivers, but you can obtain very good drivers from commercial and shareware sources in any city. Contact your local computer user's group for more information.

Installing a sys device driver just requires an entry in your CONFIG.SYS file. For example, if your driver is in a subdirectory named C:\MOUSE, you might add a line to your CONFIG.SYS file that looks like

device=C:\mouse\mouse.sys

Then, each time you reboot your computer, it installs the device driver for your mouse automatically and you do not need to worry about it again!

Installing a memory-resident mouse driver is also easy. Basically, you just type its name at the DOS prompt and press **Enter** or add an equivalent line to your AUTOEXEC.BAT file.

This probably will install a driver named mouse.com on serial port COM1. Ah ha! You caught that weasel word "probably." It's always a good idea to read the manual that comes with your mouse. Some mouse drivers default to COM1, and others must be told specifically which serial port to watch for mouse activity. Some of the newest drivers examine all your ports and locate your mouse automatically. Unfortunately, there's little standardization, so to install a driver on COM1, you might need to type one of the following and press **Enter**:

mouse

or

mouse 1

or

mouse /1

or something else, depending on your particular mouse driver. If the installation is successful, most drivers display a message that confirms

NOTE

There's a reason that most hardware accessories come with diskettes: most of them need special software, too.

NOTE

Mice rarely malfunction. This problem applies mostly to small computers such as portables, laptops, and notebook computers.

the installation and tells you the port on which they're installed (which port they're watching).

Solution #5: It may not work with your computer.

Some peripherals and most mice draw their power from the computer, through the serial port connector. This is risky because all ports are not created equal; some of them simply cannot supply the extra power. If your peripheral acts erratically, or fails to work at all, read through this chapter and apply all of our suggestions; then call your retailer and discuss the problem. You might also consider contacting your local university or computer user's group. Perhaps someone else has had the same experience.

Problem: My mouse worked fine until I rebooted my computer.

Solution: You may not have installed its driver software properly.

So, you decided to use the mouse.com file instead of the mouse.sys file. You tried it and it seemed to work at the time, so you put an entry in your AUTOEXEC.BAT and moved on to something else.

Now you've rebooted your computer and your mouse isn't working. What's wrong? Maybe the entry in your AUTOEXEC.BAT file is not quite correct. For example, if your computer reports **Bad command or file name** at boot, you may need to specify the driver's full pathname in your AUTOEXEC.BAT file, or you may have spelled something incorrectly. It never hurts to recheck your work. See also Chapter 12, "Problems with DOS and Memory," and Chapter 10, "Problems with Files."

Problem: The driver announced that it could not find my mouse.

Solution #1: Be sure your mouse is connected to your PC.

Mice receive as much abuse as keyboards because they're also attached to people! If you drop your mouse, it may become unplugged from the computer. If you use your mouse a lot, the cord may become worn or twisted, and eventually the wires inside may break.

TIP

Be sure your mouse is plugged into the port where you told the computer it would be.

If your mouse cord comes loose from your PC, it may be difficult to plug back into the correct port. The back of my PC is a tangle of cables and I hate to disturb it because it's a job to put everything back. So I find myself going through some very unusual contortions to see back there without disturbing anything.

Solution #2: Other hardware or software may be conflicting with your mouse.

Many computers have only one serial port, so people use an A/B switchbox to connect various accessories as they need them. Do you use a modem on the same port? Has someone else been using your computer?

Many serial peripherals require memory-resident software, which watches the port and handles the peripheral accessory. If someone was using a different peripheral, its software still may be installed, blocking your mouse's access to the port. Try rebooting your computer, then reinstalling your mouse and its software. If this works, discuss the problem with the other person to prevent future problems.

TIP

Memory-resident programs can conflict with each other. When in doubt, reboot and reinstall your peripheral carefully. Consider all of the equipment connected to your PC.

Problem: My mouse is acting "funny." It moves too fast, acts erratic or sluggish, or it's difficult to control.

Solution #1: You may be able to tailor the mouse action to your tastes.

Some mice come with special programs that let you set the mouse's sensitivity, both vertically and horizontally. They may have names associated with *control panels* or *speeds*. Check your mouse's manual to see if you have such a program.

Some newer applications programs include their own mouse drivers. If you use their driver instead of the one that came with your mouse, you may be able to adjust the mouse's sensitivity from within the application's setup or configuration menus.

Solution #2: Have you cleaned your mouse lately?

Everyone wants a clean mouse, right? Bet you didn't even know they could get dirty! Well, most mice have a roller ball on the underside. This ball can collect lint, food, cigarette ash, and all sorts of stuff from your desk. Eventually, it will not roll as freely as it should.

Your manual will tell you how to clean your mouse. Usually, you need to turn it over and gently twist a ring that holds the ball in the body of the mouse. Remove the ring, pop the ball out, and clean it with a soft cloth and some denatured alcohol or water. A clean roller ball will "grip," like the bottom of your new tennis shoes. While you're at it, examine the mouse and carefully remove any foreign stuff lodged in the recess where the ball rolls.

Not all mice have a roller ball; some, called *optical mice*, use light beams reflected from a special mouse pad. These mice generally have slippery feet to allow them to move freely across the pad. You may need to clean the feet or the pad occasionally, but do so carefully; use only the techniques and solvents mentioned in the mouse manual. If you damage the surface of the pad, the reflective action may not work properly.

Problem: My mouse works with some applications but not with others.

Solution: You may need to change the offending software's setup.

Mice and other serial devices are usually connected to serial ports on the back of your PC, although some come with a special card that plugs into your computer. Because you may have several serial ports, most applications that use a mouse let you configure it, or tell it which port has the mouse. You may just need to reconfigure your application for your mouse port.

In this chapter we discussed mice and other input devices and examined some of the common problems you might encounter. You learned about drivers and installation techniques and keeping a clean mouse. Now let's move on to modems and telecommunications devices. These also use your computer's serial ports, but the hardware offers more variety and the software is considerably different.

Telecommunications and Problems with Ports

Ports are your computer's doorways to the world; they carry information to or from the computer. Keyboards, printers, modems, and mice all connect to ports on your PC. In this chapter we explore ports and discuss common problems you may encounter when you set up your printer or telecommunications hardware and software.

The process of telecommunications uses a modem and a terminal to communicate over a telephone line, sort of like a remote typewriter.

What does telecommunications involve? You need a PC, a modem, and some special software—a telecommunications program.

In general, you should know that although telecommunications is one of the fastest-growing areas of PC use, it also offers the most potential for frustration, because it can involve you with hardware and software decisions simultaneously. Don't despair—it also offers the most potential for reward. You can have so much fun telecommunicating that any problems you may confront will seem inconsequential in retrospect.

Problem: I have been told by one person to connect my printer to the *printer port*, and by another to connect it to a *parallel port*. What are they, and what's the difference between them?

Solution: They are the same thing.

Ports are often named by their function—printer ports, for example. But they are also named for their architecture or how they function—serial orparallel ports, for example. Both approaches have advantages and drawbacks.

When you're setting up your PC for the first time, it helps to know which connector is the printer port. In time you may add another accessory, such as a tape backup unit, which may also hook to the printer port. The instructions for the tape drive tell you to connect it to a parallel port, so you need to know that most printer ports are generically called parallel ports.

Problem: What's a serial port? A communication port?

Solution: They are the same thing. See Chapter 2 for more information about *serial* versus *parallel* data transmission.

Problem: What are COM1 and COM2?

Solution: These are DOS names for serial communication ports.

Imagine moving into a new house. You wander around and discover where the kitchen, the bathroom, and the bedrooms are located. You find the light switches and the telephone jack in the hallway. You knew these things had to be somewhere, but now you know where they are in this house. In a sense, you "connect yourself" to your new home during this exploratory trip. You get to know where things are located.

DOS computers do the same thing every time they boot; they look around to see what's available in their new home. When they find a serial COMmunication port, they give it a number (COM1). The next port gets the next number (COM2), and so on. When you run software that needs to use a serial port, it may ask you which port it should use. Many PCs have a mouse on COM1 and a modem on COM2. Does yours?

Problem: How many serial or COM ports does my PC have?

Solution: Usually one or two. Sometimes more.

The easiest way to determine the number of ports is to read your manual or count the connectors on the back of your machine. Serial ports can be 25-pin male or 9-pin male DB connectors.

There are many *utility programs* that examine your PC and produce a report about your system, including the number of installed serial ports. You also can use the program named DEBUG that came with your computer to find out how many serial ports you have, but doing so is way beyond the scope of this book. If you really need to know, contact your retailer or local PC user's group for help.

Problem: I have a mouse, a scanner, and have now purchased a modem. I need to have a third serial port; how do I do it?

Solution: You can use up to four ports fairly easily, but you may need special software for the last two, COM3 and COM4.

First, a serial port is a piece of hardware, usually a plug-in card. Some PCs have multifunction cards that include a printer port and one or two serial ports. And the hardware is not the whole story. You also need software to drive the port. DOS provides the most basic type of port handlers, but most serial devices (mice, modems, etc.) provide special software to enhance the product.

DOS still cannot accommodate more than two ports easily, even though DOS 5.0 offered some improvements. Various equipment manufacturers have figured out how to add multiple serial ports to personal computers, but their solutions seldom work with every computer because DOS fundamentally does not support it.

The best solution seems to be to switch your various serial devices among the ports that you do have. You can buy a special "A/B" switch box for this purpose.

Problem: My scanner installation instructions tell me to select an *interrupt* or *IRQ*. What are they, and should I care about them?

Solution: An interrupt is a way of getting the computer's attention so it can handle chores that occur at unexpected times.

Computers actually do only one thing at a time, such as running your favorite word processor. Occasionally, though, they need to take care of something unexpected, such as answering the phone.

You really don't need to understand why the PC has interrupts, but you do need to know that some of them affect your serial ports. In general, COM1 or COM3 should be assigned to IRQ4 (interrupt #4) and COM2 or COM4 should be paired with IRQ3. Other interrupts affect your parallel ports. Parallel ports should use IRQ5 or IRQ7.

Problem: My mouse is connected to a serial port, and it's not working.

Solution: You may have a port *conflict* with other hardware.

Serial ports can do only one thing at a time. Many people have discovered that internal modems are seen by the computer as ports, too. If you are using a mouse and an external modem, you already have discovered the need for two serial ports because you need two connectors. But if you have an internal modem, you must be sure that it is not set to the same address and corresponding interrupt as the serial port for your mouse. Your PC cannot tell which is which unless they have unique addresses and interrupt settings.

Try removing the modem and rebooting your PC. If the mouse works, you have a port conflict. It's usually a good idea to put the mouse on COM1 because many software packages that use mice insist upon this. The mouse software automatically selects the IRQ4 interrupt. Then put your modem on COM2 and set it for IRQ3.

See also Chapter 6, "Problems with Mice and Scanners."

Problem: The setup instructions for my telecommunications hardware talk about *DTE* and *DCE*. What are they?

Solution: Computers (ports) are generally DTE, Data Transmission Equipment, and modems should be DCE, Data Communications Equipment. See the Glossary for more information.

Problem: The telecommunications software wants me to select a *terminal emulation*. What's that and what should I choose?

Solution: You usually should choose IBM PC or ANSI emulation.

Computers are very good at pretending to be other devices. Before PCs became popular, folks used dedicated computer terminals to operate big mainframe computers. These terminals each had their own way of communicating with the mainframes.

When you select a terminal emulation, you are telling your computer to act like a particular brand or type of terminal, usually because the system you're communicating with expects it.

When in doubt, select a generic emulation such as ANSI, then change it after you've connected to the remote computer and watch what happens to the display on your screen. If you get garbage, you can change back "on the fly" (without losing the connection to the remote computer).

Problem: My telecommunications software is asking for a baud rate (or "BPS"). Which value should I choose?

Solution: This depends upon your modem and whom you're calling.

Do you know someone who talks really fast, or v e r y s l o w l y? Is it hard to understand them? Sometimes the speed with which we talk can make communication difficult, for people or computers. The BAUD rate (or BPS) determines how fast your computer communicates with another computer, or any serial peripheral. Unlike people, computers can only communicate if they are both using exactly the same rate.

Actually BAUD is an outdated term that refers to a specific company's serial communication scheme. The correct term is "bits per second" or BPS and they are not strictly the same measure, but you may see the two used interchangeably. So, what does BPS mean?

We've all heard our parents S-P-E-L-L words at Christmastime, to avoid giving away any secrets about the P-R-E-S-E-N-T-S. That is a form of serial communication. The listener hears the letters, then reassembles them into words to get the true meaning.

Computers deal with BYTES of information and each byte has eight BITS. A BIT is the smallest unit of information in a computer, just like the letters in the words our parents spelled over our heads. But a BIT can only be a "1" or a "0" because computers use electronic circuits that are either On or OFF. When a computer sends a byte in serial fashion, it sends a stream of eight bits (ones or zeros or a mixture, depending upon the byte).

When we talk, we generally pause between sentences, to help our listeners digest our message. Computers do the same thing. The sending computer interposes STOP BITS between the informational bits, like our pauses. The receiving computer uses the STOP BITS as a guide and reassembles the ones and zeros into the original bytes.

So, BAUD (or BPS) is a measure of how fast our computers send and receive the individual bits that form the bytes that form our messages. Whew!

With baud rates (and BPS), bigger is better and faster. It's also cheaper when you're calling long-distance! But your modem hardware sets the upper limit on the BPS you can use. Most modems can only communicate at rates up to 2400 BPS, although some newer units can achieve 9600 (or greater) speeds.

If you're using a modem to call another computer or a bulletin board or any piece of electronic gadgetry, ask the person in charge of that equipment for its BPS, PARITY, and the number of STOP BITS to use, then set up your telecommunications package the same way. See the next problem/solution, or the Glossary, for additional definitions of BAUD, BPS, PARITY, and STOP BITS.

Above all, don't be afraid to experiment. The worst that will happen is that you won't make a successful connection the first time. This just makes it more satisfying when you finally do connect!

Problem: OK, now my telecommunications software wants to know what *parity* I want.

Solution: Parity concerns the pattern of information sent along a serial communications link—your telephone, for example. It's a very simple error-checking mechanism that comes in several flavors.

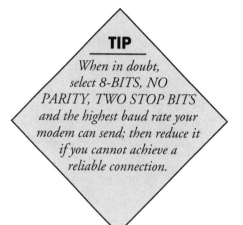

TIP

When in doubt, select 8-BITS, NO PARITY, TWO STOP BITS and the highest baud rate your modem can send; then reduce it if you cannot achieve a reliable connection.

Consider the teacher who takes her class to the zoo. She came with fifteen children, so she won't leave with fewer than fifteen! The class count is her way of checking for errors. (But if that were the only criteria, she might take the wrong kids home . . .)

Parity works much like the teacher's scheme. It concerns the quantity of bits sent in each byte. It can be odd, even, or totally ignored (no parity). And it's only a count; unlike the teacher who can see her kids, it cannot detect wrong bits.

When in doubt, select **No parity**, then change it if you see garbage. Again, don't be afraid to experiment. The worst that will happen is that you'll connect successfully but then see garbage on your screen. You can change the parity without losing the connection, too.

Problem: My telecommunications software is asking me to select the number of *stop bits*.

Solution: Choose **None**, then change later if necessary.

The number of stop bits you need depends on whom you're calling. Various systems are set up to require none, one, or two, at the operator's discretion. Don't be afraid to experiment. The worst that will happen is that you'll connect successfully but then see garbage on your screen. You can change the number of stop bits without losing the connection.

Problem: I've done everything I'm supposed to, and my modem still doesn't work.

Solution: Is it properly connected to your PC? Properly powered?

External modems must be connected to computers by a data cable. Has your cable come loose? External modems usually also require AC power. Does your modem have a power cord or a "wall knocker" adapter? Is it connected? Plug a lamp into the same socket to see if it has power.

And last but not least, all modems must connect to a telephone line. This little cable is far more fragile than any of the other cables in your system. Is your modem securely connected to the telephone line? Try connecting a standard telephone to the same jack, with the same cable. Do you hear a dial tone?

Problem: How can I really tell if my modem is working properly?

Solution #1: If you are using an external modem, watch its lights.

Many external modems have a series of light emitting diodes (LEDs) on the front of the case. To see if your computer is talking to your modem, run your favorite telecommunications program and select a very slow baud rate (300 or below).

Watch the modem's lights while repeatedly pressing any keyboard key. You should see the modem's TX (transmit) LED flicker as each character reaches the modem. Generally, your modem does not need to be connected to the telephone for this test.

If you have an internal modem, there are utility software packages that put cute little symbols on your screen to show you the modem's status, as if they were LEDs on an imaginary front panel.

Solution #2: Use one of its built-in commands.

Some of the first "smart" modems for PCs were marketed by the Hayes™ Company. They forged a new path that others followed, with "Hayes-compatible" products. These modems contain a built-in set of commands that your PC uses to provide the modern telecommunication activity we have come to consider normal.

> **CAUTION**
>
> *Some utility software can cause as many problems as it solves, because it is one more thing for your computer to do, at a time when it's already busy with the modem!*

If your modem is "Hayes-compatible," you can "ask it if it's listening to you" (query it), and if it is, it will respond to you in a particular way. This test will work with both internal and external "Hayes-compatible" modems.

To test this, start up your telecommunications software. Type **at** and press **Enter**. If everything is connected properly, your modem will respond with **OK**, telling you that your modem is connected and waiting for you to tell it to dial the phone.

Problem: I get the **OK**, now how do I make my modem dial the telephone?

Solution: There are three general ways to dial a telephone.

First, if you have a Hayes-compatible modem, you can use its built-in commands to dial the telephone. Most modems are Hayes-compatible. To dial your phone, start your telecommunications software. When you're in its terminal mode, type **atdpxxx-xxxx** and press **Enter**. Substitute the number you wish to dial for the **xxx-xxxx**.

Another way to dial the phone depends on your telecommunications software. Many packages include a dialer feature, much like your phone book. You must enter each number once, then you just call up the dialer and select an entry; it will be dialed for you.

The last way to dial the phone is with your finger. When the ringing begins, be sure your system is "off hook," then hang up the receiver.

Problem: My modem has just stopped working.

Solution: Has someone in another room picked up an extension phone?

Modems do not like party lines. They get grumpy and display strange characters on your screen when someone in another room lifts the receiver, unaware that you are using the line. Is your line secure?

Problem: What's a *host mode?* What's an *auto-answer mode?*

Solution: These are modes that allow your computer to answer the phone.

So far, we've discussed only the case in which you place a call; the *originate mode* of operation. Host mode is an advanced form of operation that will let your friends call you. But there's a potential problem here; someone you don't like could call and damage your software or data files.

Problem: I want to download a file from a bulletin board. What *protocol* should I use?

Solution: The safest choice is the XMODEM protocol, BINARY format.

TIP

Be very careful when using host mode or auto-answer features on your system. You will be letting other people access your data!

A protocol is a method of moving information. It makes the computers on each end agree on how many bytes to send at a time, how to tell if the packet was received intact, and what to do about damaged packets.

81

XMODEM is only one of several protocols in common use. Because it's one of the oldest, most systems do it correctly. After you've gotten comfortable moving files around, you can try other protocols to see which works fastest and most reliably in your part of the country.

Choosing the BINARY format warns your system not to change or filter out any characters in the file. If you are downloading a purely ASCII text file, with no embedded formatting, choosing an ASCII format is fine, but much slower.

And of course, all these tips also apply to uploading files.

Problem: How can I make my modem hang up the phone?

Solution: There's always a way . . .

Your telecommunications software probably provides a special key combination to disconnect or terminate a call. If your modem is Hayes-compatible, typing **ath** and pressing **Enter** usually will hang up the phone.

If your modem is not Hayes-compatible, read your manual; there's always an instruction to do this important task. As a last resort, just disconnect the phone cord from the wall. It's no big deal, as long as you remember to reconnect it before someone calls to tell you that you've won a $10,000,000 jackpot!

In this chapter, we explored the most common problems you might encounter with ports and telecommunications software. Now let's look at printers and investigate your printing needs.

Problems with Printers and Fonts

If your computer didn't provide you with a way to get your ideas and thoughts in front of someone else, computing would be reduced to a rather expensive solitaire game. A simple thing like printing a letter starts a complex chain of events that begins at your keyboard and ends (you hope) on the paper. Along the way you depend upon the computer, software, cables, printer, and, ultimately, the paper. If even one link in this chain fails, the whole process can become a frustrating mess. Fortunately, once you get the links in place, they are not inclined to move!

Let's assume that you've already checked your cables and connectors. You know that your printer is properly hooked up, turned on, and on-line. If you haven't done this, refer to Chapter 3, "Problems with Cables and Connectors."

In this chapter, we approach printing the way it evolved, from simple to not-so-simple. We explore some solutions to basic problems, then move ahead to more complex issues. If you approach your system in the same way, you'll be printing again in no time!

Problem: My software manual says that I need to have an IBM-compatible printer. How do I find out if I do?

Solution: Look in your printer manual or check with your retailer.

Chances are that it is compatible, especially if you've been using it successfully. Most printers sold with PCs today are compatible; the real problems arise when we try to use their advanced features from within applications programs like spreadsheets and word processors.

Switches and Switch Settings

Everyone knows what an electrical switch is. Your house has lots of them. They make or break electrical circuits. Your overhead lights are a good example. But not all switches control your lights and not all carry large AC voltages. Some, like the little bitty ones in your computer system, are "logic switches" that determine how your system behaves.

TIP

Check new PC accessory manuals for default settings. If actual settings vary, write them down, and then try factory settings first.

PC peripherals seem to have more little switches than other types of equipment. If they're set correctly, you may never know that they exist. And incorrect settings should do no permanent damage; your system simply won't function as you wish. You should know that products usually come from the factory with the switches already placed in the proper (default) position.

If you do change a switch-setting, note the change in the equipment's manual (or your logbook) for future reference. I use a pencil for these notes because then I can erase it if I subsequently change the settings.

These switches are often so small that you must use a pen or other stylus to move them. They are called "dip" switches because they fit into "dip" (Dual In-line Plug) sockets, although some folks think the designers were "dips" for using them . . . Many of the small, black "chips" scattered across your computer's circuit boards are actually plugged into "dip" sockets, to facilitate easy repair.

Problem: I can't locate my printer's switches.

Solution: Look in the manual that came with the printer.

No, the switches aren't in the manual, but it should tell you where to find them. Not all printers have setup switches but if they do, they are generally located on the back, the bottom, or inside of the printer, along the front. You may need to pull off a cover or open a door to see them. If you are convinced they exist but you just can't find them, contact your retailer, warranty service center, or PC user's group for help.

TIP

Treat dip switches carefully; they are fragile. Use an old pen or a dull stylus to change them and expect to "feel" the "click" that occurs when they toggle.

TIP

Be sure to turn your printer OFF before changing any switch settings. This is good for you and the printer!

Problem: I don't understand my printer's switch settings.

Solution: Look in the manual that came with the printer.

First, the printer came to you with the switches set somehow! These were probably the factory "default" settings we discussed earlier. You should only need to change them occasionally. If your printer has switches, they will be described in its manual but the terms may be unfamiliar, so let's examine a few of the common ones:

MODE settings   Many printers can "act" like other brands of printers. When one brand becomes popular, other manufacturers give their products a "mode" to mimic it. You may see mode choices like "IBM Proprinter" or "Epson RX-80," for example.

CHARACTER SET settings   Many printers can produce characters in several "fonts" and sizes. You can select the printer's font and/or font-size with these switches. Usually, you can also download new font sets from your computer without changing these switch settings. The settings usually only specify the printer's "initial" font (the font it uses when first turned on).

PITCH settings   This can be misleading. A font's "pitch" is the space between characters, but in some printers this setting actually determines whether you obtain normal or BOLD printing. See your manual.

AUTO FEED settings   Sometimes you want the printer to automatically advance the paper one line when it's printed a complete line. At other times, your applications software will take care of this detail for you. The AUTO FEED setting lets you select how the printer handles the situation when its carriage reaches the right edge of the paper.

SKIP PERFORATION setting   Sometimes you want the printer to stop printing near (but not at) the bottom of the paper, advance the paper past the perforation, then continue printing on the next sheet. The alternative is to let the printer just keep on printing right over the perforation between pages and onto the next sheet. Most word processing software packages handle this detail for you, but you may occasionally want to use this setting to force the printer to skip the perforated areas.

TIP

After you change any settings, you may need to reboot your computer so it can "discover" the changes.

In this section, we've listed only a few of the possible uses for switches in PC printers. But you now have an idea of their diversity.

Problem: My printer is not printing, is printing oddly, or is printing garbage.

Solution: You may need to reset it.

Printers can operate in several modes. The newer ones can switch between their normal command sets and special Postscript commands. If it's in the wrong mode, it may not recognize your commands.

Did you have a power failure or a loose cable that caused a premature exit from an application? Has someone else been using the printer with a new program?

Know how to reset your printer. Look in the manual that came with your printer to find out how to reset it to its native mode. You may only need to switch it off and back on again, or you may need to use its keypad to put it in a special mode that matches the software you're using.

Problem: My printer will not print.

Solution: Will it run its "internal self-test"?

Most printers have an internal "self-test" feature. You usually can invoke it by pressing a combination of buttons on the printer while turning it off and back on. Expect to see it print its entire character set or something similar. If the printer successfully completes its self-test, it's probably working fine. Refer to your printer's manual for information about its self-test.

Problem: My printer is beeping at me.

Solution #1: It may be out of paper.

Many printers will beep to attract your attention when they run out of paper. They may also have a light or LED on their front panel to indicate this condition.

Some printers have a switch that you can set to tell the computer to ignore the "paper-out" sensor. You might want to use it if you were using sheets of paper instead of fan-fold paper. But you'd have to be careful to print only one page at a time.

Solution #2: It may have overheated.

Some printers have an internal heat sensor to stop them if they get too hot. When they stop, they beep. Evidently, these printers can overheat if you use them continuously. I've never seen one do that, but it sounds expensive. If possible, I'd buy one without the sensor because it seems like an admission of a problem.

Of course, paper is very dusty stuff, so your printer may become clogged with paper dust. Every few months, you should clean it out according to the directions in the manual. Perhaps this was the thinking behind the "overheat" sensor. Dust could act as insulation and hold the heat in the printer.

Problem: My printer is printing in the wrong place on each page.

Solution: You must align the paper in your printer before you start printing.

This can be a problem with printers that use fan-fold computer paper, but it's not usually a problem with sheet-fed printers.

If you are using fan-fold printer paper, you probably need to roll the paper through the printer until it is aligned with the print head, before turning your printer ON. Your manual should explain how to do this. Look for a knob on one side of your printer. Turn the knob to move the paper.

TIP

You should never FORCE the paper-advance knob to turn when the printer is on! The best procedure is to always turn the printer OFF before twisting the paper-advance knob.

Some printers have a "top of form" button you can press to tell them that the paper is now properly positioned. Your manual should explain this, too.

Once you have the paper aligned, you really should not need to realign it until you change the paper. If you find yourself continually readjusting the paper, something is not set up correctly. Check your printer manual and the guides that came with your applications software to identify the conflict.

Printing Files from the DOS Command Line

Problem: I need to tell my software where to find my printer (what port it is on). How can I find out?

Solution #1: Print your name (and answer your question).

DOS, without the aid of word processing software, offers three different ways to print files. You can COPY information to a printer port, use the PRINT command, or do a *screen dump* (print the information presently displayed on your monitor).

Printer ports are parallel ports located on your computer. They have strange DOS names like "LPT1:" and "LPT2:". LPT means LinePrinTer, and each one is assigned a number, beginning with one.

To find which port your printer is connected to, try this simple exercise:

1. From the DOS prompt, type

   copy con: lpt1:

   This redirects everything you type to a buffer in your computer. Notice that there are spaces between **copy**, **con:**, and **lpt1:**.

2. Type your name, then press **Enter**.

3. Press **Ctrl-Z** (the Ctrl key and the Z key at the same time) to stop the buffering process.

4. Press **Enter** again, to print the contents of the buffer.

If your printer is connected to LPT1:, turned on, and on-line, it should have printed your name! And notice that the Ctrl-Z key combination produced the ^Z characters on your screen.

If your PC gives you an error message such as

**Write fault error writing device LPT1
Abort, Retry, Ignore, Fail?**

it's telling you that the printer is connected to that port but it's either turned off, off-line, or out of paper. And it's asking you if you wish to

Abort the process

Retry the process

Ignore the error

Fail (another type of abort) the process

Type **a** to abort the process, then correct your printer and try this test again. If nothing happens, repeat the four steps in the exercise, but use **lpt2** as the destination. Most printers are attached to LPT1: or LPT2:, so you should easily establish if your printer is functioning and to which port it's connected.

Solution #2: Use ASCII (text) files.

The next example shows you how to do it with a file named CONFIG.SYS, but you can also COPY your AUTOEXEC.BAT file (or any other ASCII file) to your printer in this manner.

At the DOS prompt, type

copy config.sys lpt1:

Notice that this takes much less typing than the method shown above, but you must have an ASCII file to print. You may need to use **lpt2:** or even **lpt3:**. If you get any of the error messages described under Solution #1, you should take the same corrective actions described there.

Now you know where your printer is located. And you can print your name as well as simple files!

Problem: Whenever I try to print anything my computer says **Bad command or filename**.

Solution: Ensure that the PRINT.EXE program exists on your system, located where DOS can find it.

If your PC says **Bad command or filename**, it's trying to do what you asked but cannot find the PRINT.EXE file, so it doesn't know how to do it. You will see this message whenever you issue a command that DOS does not recognize. I see it a lot when I type **dit** instead of **dir** because the two keys are adjacent on my keyboard and I am not the world's best typist!

DOS would be pretty worthless if it didn't provide a way to print files, so the designers included the PRINT.EXE program. Unfortunately, people occasionally set up their systems without this important file; or it may have been accidentally deleted. You must be sure this file is somewhere where DOS can find it. The best way to accomplish this is to include it in the DOS PATH statement. The DOS PATH statement tells your PC where to look for programs and files.

The DOS PATH is usually established at boot by an entry in your AUTOEXEC.BAT file. For simplicity, many folks install all their DOS programs in a hard drive subdirectory named DOS (actually, on hard drives it's usually named C:\DOS), so that's a good place to look for the PRINT.EXE program.

The easiest way to see if PRINT.EXE is in your PATH is to ask DOS to show you the current PATH. At the DOS command prompt, type **path** and press **Enter**.

You should see something like

PATH=C:\;C:\DOS;C:\UTILS;

Notice that this is just a list of subdirectories, separated by semicolons. On my system, the PRINT.EXE program is located in the C:\DOS subdirectory. If your PC has a PATH similar to the example above, look for the PRINT.EXE program in one of those subdirectories.

If instead of a path, your PC says it has

No Path

you may have a setup problem or you may have booted to a disk which has no AUTOEXEC.BAT file. See Chapter 12, "Problems with DOS and Memory," for more information.

In any event, if you absolutely cannot locate the PRINT.EXE program, reinstall it from your DOS distribution diskettes. Although it's not considered good housekeeping, it's okay to have several copies of this program on your system, but they must all be from the same version of DOS!

When you are sure that PRINT.EXE is in your PATH or in your current directory, you should no longer see this error message because DOS will be able to find the PRINT command. But it may not be able to find your file, as in the next problem.

Problem: I want to print a file but my PC reports **File not found.**

Solution: You may be spelling or using its name incorrectly.

Are you trying to print filename when the real name is filename.doc? Remember that unlike you and me, DOS does not understand nicknames! DOS filenames adhere to a strict structure. They may have one or two parts, separated by a period. The first part can have no more than eight characters, the second a maximum of three. Space characters and most punctuation marks are not allowed.

In the best of all worlds we couldn't violate these naming conventions. However, some word processors will (apparently) let you create files with invalid names, and you may not find this out until you try to access the file and find that it's missing!

Some invalid filenames are my.letter, letter.to.mom, or yesterday's.news, or .doc.

Some valid examples are letter.doc, text.mom, mom_1.doc, or yestrday.txt.

Can you see why these names are right or wrong? See your DOS manual for additional information on filename syntax.

Problem: My computer keeps asking me **Name of list device [PRN]**.

Solution: The easy answer here is to simply press **Enter**.

Your computer will send all printing to the default PRN: logical device until you reboot. If you have several printers or if your printer is on LPT2:, you need to type **lpt2:**, then press **Enter**.

This question was intended by the DOS designers as a way to select among several printer ports at boot. All versions of DOS will ask this question unless you include a special command in your AUTOEXEC.BAT file.

Notice that DOS only asks you this question once, the first time you print something after booting. Then it remembers your choice and doesn't bother you about it again until you reboot.

Problem: I want to print what's on my computer screen. How do I do it?

Solution: Use the **Shift-PrintScreen** key combination.

If this command works, your printer should immediately begin printing whatever characters are on-screen at the moment. If this happens, you know that your hardware is connected correctly. If this command does not work, don't despair, just read on . . .

Problem: The Shift-PrintScreen command prints garbage.

Solution: You may need to issue the DOS GRAPHICS command.

NOTE

*The DOS screen dump doesn't work on most laser printers. One of the simplest ways to print something is to press **Shift-PrintScreen** at the DOS prompt.*

Remember that we're still discussing how to print from the DOS command line. DOS does not innately understand graphics characters, but it does include a special program named GRAPHICS.COM to handle these chores for some display modes and printers. See your DOS manual for information about the GRAPHICS command.

To test this idea, type **graphics** at the DOS prompt and press **Enter**. Notice that your hard drive light illuminates for a moment, then the DOS prompt returns. When this happens, DOS has just installed the

GRAPHICS program as a TSR, enabling you to do screen dumps to most nonlaser printers and using up some of your precious 640K of RAM with no warning!

Printing Files from Within Applications

An application is a program, like a text editor or a word processor. In the PC world it's the hardware and the applications programs that provide the desirable effects we associate with desktop publishing and printing.

You need to know some terms before we continue. You've heard of *fonts* and *typefaces* and *points* but what do they mean? They are traditional printer terms to describe sets of characters. (See Figure 8.1.)

A font or typeface is a collection of characters that resemble each other. They are available in various sizes. For example:

This line is printed with a twelve point Helvetica font.

This line is printed with a nine point Helvetica bold font.

`This line is printed in ten point Courier font.`

The names for most fonts are copyrighted, so you may see essentially the same thing described as Helvetica, or Helios, or any of dozens of other names.

A point is a measure of vertical size. In the example above, the twelve point font was taller than the ten point one.

American Typewriter (6 point)

Bodoni (8 point)

Helvetica (10 point)

Helvetica (12 point)

Helvetica (14 point)

Goudy (16 point)

Times (18 point)

MCP Digital (20 point)

Bookman (22 point)

Figure 8.1 PC users have a choice of typestyles and fonts.

Problem: I can't find my fonts, where are they? In the printer? In software?

Solution: Both places, actually.

First, let's discuss traditional, non-Postscript printing. In order to print a character of a certain font and size, the application must be able to specify the font and the printer must be able to reproduce it on demand. You make these choices when you create the document, and your printer supports them during printing.

When DOS was first released, the designers anticipated the need for a variety of graphic effects, so they gave it a graphic display capability as well as the traditional text display mode. But economics caused the applications software and the printer hardware to lag behind our desires. (So, what else is new?) For several years, we were restricted to the fonts that were actually built into our printers, accessible in text mode. Graphics mode printing was possible but very, very slow and loaded with pitfalls.

Eventually, printers were given the ability to receive files of custom fonts from the PC. You could download a *soft font*, a reference file you load into your PC, to your printer, but you were restricted to using only that font.

More recently, windowing software has begun operating mostly in the DOS graphic mode. The driving forces here are our demands for better resolution and more flexibility, combined with the availability of faster processors and competition among software manufacturers.

Modern printers still contain several character sets for text mode printing, but some (notably laser and laser-quality printers) also respond to a new printer-control language called Postscript. These printers can reproduce virtually any shape the software asks for.

Newer applications programs are now available with soft fonts. When you use one of these programs, you can specify any of the fonts you have installed. The font specifications are contained (embedded) within your datafile (a letter you write, for example) and sent to the printer when you print the letter.

Problem: My file prints oddly—it seems to contain weird characters.

Solution: You may be printing it in the wrong way.

Earlier in this chapter, we discussed printing files from the DOS command line. Unfortunately, this is not a universal method because of the embedded print formatting commands mentioned above. Although applications programs can now create special effects, there are few standards, so your best bet is to print a file from within the application that created it.

You should use the DOS PRINT command only for files that contain pure ASCII text. If you print a file created with a word processor, your printer may have trouble with the special specifications that your word processor embedded in the file. Fortunately, most applications will let you save a file in one of several formats. One of these is usually pure ASCII, but you'll often lose the special effects that you labored so long to create.

This same problem presents itself when you try to view a file. There are special file viewing programs that can translate a variety of embedded printer commands for display purposes, but again your best bet is to view the file from within the application that created it.

Problem: I want to use a font called Benguait, but my application does not offer it.

Solution: You may need to add the font to your application.

If you are using a word processor that operates in the text mode, you will be able to specify only fonts and effects that exist in your printer. See your printer's manual for a listing. You may need to run your application's INSTALLATION or SETUP program to tell it which printer you're using and how to access that printer's features. Or you may need to download a soft font to your printer.

If you are using a newer word processor that operates in the graphics mode, you may be able to install additional fonts but you still need to be aware of your printer's limitations, and you may need to purchase the additional fonts from your retailer. Then you need to run your application's INSTALLATION or SETUP program to tell it about the new fonts. See your application's manual(s) or contact your retailer for more details.

Problem: My application is complaining that it cannot find a font.

Solution: You may need to reinstall the font on the system you're using.

Did you create the document on that system? With that software? If you create a document on one system, it may not be displayable (or printable) on another system unless both have the same applications programs with the same fonts — and perhaps the same printers — installed.

Problem: My document prints oddly on different computer systems.

Solution: You may need to update your software or restrict your formats.

Did you create the document on that system? With that software? If you create a document on one system, with one version of an application, it may not display or print correctly on another system unless both have the same version of the applications programs, with the same fonts — and perhaps the same printers — installed. Whew!

The problem here is that old software doesn't know about newer features. For example, if you use a new version of a program and specify a ten point font in your document, an older version may not understand that specification. The results can be amazing. This also could apply to tab settings, margins, or any other type of formatting.

See Chapter 13, "Problems with Software," for more information.

TIP

If you must remain compatible among various systems, learn features of the oldest version of the application software first. Avoid using newer features until you upgrade.

In this chapter, we discussed printers and fonts and several ways to print your files, from DOS and from applications. You learned how to identify your ports by number and what to do when you get certain error messages.

Now let's look at some problems you may encounter with your video display. You'll see that these problems can be quite similar to printer problems because a printer is really just a form of display. However, the folks who manufacture video systems and those who make printers have solved the same problems in different ways.

Problems with Video Displays

The Chinese proverb that states one picture is worth more than a thousand words must have been coined with today's computer displays in mind. In fact, fully one-third of the cost of most computer systems is devoted to the display.

In Chapter 6, you learned that mice need special software to do their job. Here you learn that even though video systems involve a bit more hardware, they need the same kind of special software, too. But you have many more opportunities to tailor the system to your tastes.

Problem: My manuals talk about all kinds of different display resolutions. I just want to get a monitor that will perform well with my software. What do I look for?

Solution: Buy the best monitor you can afford and try it before you buy it.

Video systems undergo constant improvement. This means that today's gee-whiz performance can be found on tomorrow's closeout table. But that's not necessarily bad, and that closeout special may be just what you want. The key is to establish how much resolution you need for best results with the application software you will be using, and buy to that level.

If you are interested in tech-y hardware stuff, there are lots of things to know about video systems. For example, your system's total performance depends upon such factors as

● The monitor's horizontal and vertical *bandwidth*

● The screen's *dot pitch*

● The size of the screen, measured diagonally

● The speed of your computer, in megahertz

● The amount of RAM memory in your computer

● The amount of memory on your video card

● Which set of chips your video card includes

● The combination of software you're using

All you really need to do is see the system run your favorite combination of software before you buy it. Try to ensure that the lighting is similar to yours, and plan to spend at least thirty minutes in front of the computer. Be on the lookout for signs of eyestrain, like headaches or a nervous, jittery feeling. If you experience them, try a display with a higher resolution.

Problem: My video card manual brags about being noninterlaced. Is this a big deal?

Solution: It depends upon the software you use.

If you are running any software that is graphically intense—shows more than just text on the screen—you may want to avoid monitors that have interlaced display modes.

Interlaced means that the picture is painted on the screen every other line at a time. When the picture reaches the end of the screen, it then goes back and fills in the blanks. This method of display often results in a monitor that flickers. Although you may not notice it at first, this can be hard on your eyes and your disposition.

The easy way to tell if your system is interlaced is to look at the price tag. High-resolution, noninterlaced monitors are substantially more expensive.

Problem: What does video memory do?

Solution: It stores the picture while it is being displayed.

Video memory is important because it relieves your computer of the time-consuming task of updating or "refreshing" the display. This is RAM memory located on your video card; it's different

TIP

When a salesman wows you with big numbers like "1024 x 768," ask if the system is interlaced or noninterlaced at that resolution. If it's interlaced, take a long look before buying.

111

than cache, extended, expanded, or 640K memory. Buy as much video memory as you can afford—you won't be sorry. And don't plan on a later upgrade; the amount of memory on most video cards is fixed at the time of manufacture.

TIP

Choose the resolution you need by noting the resolutions your software recommends for best results. Then buy a system that is non-interlaced at those resolutions.

Problem: Should I worry about *bus width?*

Solution: Yes—bigger is faster and better.

Bus width is the number of bits of information the video card can receive from your computer at one time. For best results your computer must be able to write to the card very swiftly. Be sure to ask whether the card you're considering buying allows 8-bit or 16-bit transfers. Bigger numbers are better.

Hardware Problems

Problem: My monitor's connector does not match my computer.

Solution: You may just need a simple adapter or you may be about to make an expensive mistake!

Various video systems require different connectors, but there are only three or four types. Generally, each substantial video improvement (like the move from EGA to VGA) has introduced a new connector style.

You can buy inexpensive adaptors to surmount this problem, but you should consider why you need the adaptor. Some newer video cards can overdrive (ruin) some older monitors. At the least, you won't get the performance you expect. It's always best to use the appropriate monitor and video card together; the connectors should match. Check your manuals or ask your retailer before you connect an old monitor to a new card.

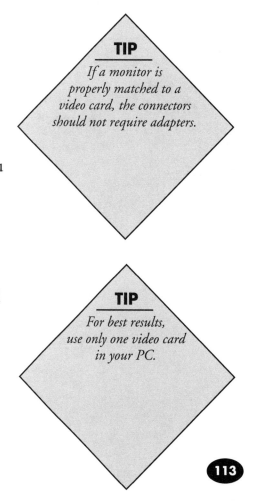

TIP

If a monitor is properly matched to a video card, the connectors should not require adapters.

Problem: I installed a new video card and it does not work.

Solution: Did you disable or remove the old one?

Most video cards expect to be the only such card in your PC. If you mix them, they can create address conflicts with the other video cards and perhaps with other peripherals that use your computer's RAM memory.

TIP

For best results, use only one video card in your PC.

They will not be happy and they will not work properly! There are exceptions, but you'll know them by the price.

Problem: I booted my PC, but there's no picture on the display.

Solution #1: Video monitors must be cabled to the computer. Is yours?

Oh, boy! Here's another opportunity for me to harp about cables and connectors. Be sure that the cable from your monitor to your video card is securely fastened and in good repair.

> **CAUTION**
>
> *Always turn your computer and your monitor off before disconnecting or reconnecting video cables.*

Solution #2: Video monitors usually have a separate on/off switch. Is your monitor turned on?

Problem: My video monitor is making a high-pitched whine.

Solution: Turn your system off—NOW!

If you turn on your system and hear a high-pitched whine, your monitor may be operating at the wrong frequency, and if it goes on for too long you may wind up having to replace the monitor. Check to ensure that your video board is set to match your monitor.

See the manuals that came with your system or contact your retailer if you are unsure how to set up your system.

If your system has been operating normally until now, your monitor may be dusty. Video monitors contain a high-voltage power supply.

Like your television set, monitors are not dangerous unless you open their cabinets.

Unfortunately, that high-voltage power supply also attracts dust, which can degrade the electronics and cause an annoying whine or an expensive breakdown. A dirty system with a whine is heading for trouble, and the whine can be very annoying to folks with acute hearing. Consider having your entire system cleaned at least annually, or more often if you notice a major accumulation of dust on the backs of the cabinets.

CAUTION

Don't open your monitor unless you know what you're doing! You run the risk of shocking yourself and ruining your monitor. And opening up your monitor almost always voids your warranty.

Problem: My display is acting like a bad TV set: rolling or showing horizontal bars.

Solution: You may need to adjust your monitor.

Computer monitors are basically TV sets without the receiver. They have controls for horizontal and vertical stability, color and the other attributes you'd expect. Of course, some monitors do not give you easy access to these controls. If your monitor is acting up, a cookie monster may have twiddled whatever controls are available.

Video Driver Problems

Problem: How do I install the software for my new video system?

Solution: Carefully!

It may seem challenging, but it's actually easy! The best way to install the software is to boot your computer from a floppy diskette and get the new software working there, before changing any of the files on your hard drive!

When you buy a newer, fancier video system, it will come with special video device driver software. If you install this driver, your computer will use it to give you much better video performance.

Most video cards come with a diskette, which usually contains three kinds of software: video diagnostics, a generic software driver, and other special device drivers tailored for specific programs—spreadsheets, computer-aided design packages, or Windows.

> **CAUTION**
>
> *Use installation programs carefully. Copy everything that might be damaged onto a diskette before using any automatic installation program. Better safe than sorry!*

You should install the software device drivers that enhance your system's video performance. Fortunately, it's easy to do. First, read the manual that came with your video card and look for a "readme" file on the new diskette. If the diskette contains an installation program, it probably will do most of the work for you. But be sure to see Chapter 13, "Problems with Software," before you run the installation program.

To install the driver, just follow these simple steps:

1. Prepare a bootable floppy diskette for your A: drive. (See the section about formatting a diskette in your

DOS manual.) Basically, you need to use the DOS FORMAT command with the /S option to format a diskette in your A: drive.

2. Your new device driver will have a name that ends with .SYS. Copy it to the bootable diskette. You may need to copy it from the distribution diskette to your hard drive, then from the hard drive to your bootable diskette. To be sure I don't accidentally erase or overwrite my existing video driver, I usually make a subdirectory named **JUNK** on my hard drive and do all of my copying to/from there. When I'm finished, I remove the JUNK subdirectory at my leisure.

3. Use EDLIN or a word processor to create a file named **CONFIG.SYS** on the bootable diskette. You must store this file in a pure ASCII format, not in the word processor's special storage format. (See your DOS manual for more information about EDLIN and CONFIG.SYS.)

4. Add the following line to your new CONFIG.SYS file:

   device=NEWDRIVER.SYS

   but substitute your driver's actual filename for the words **NEWDRIVER.SYS.**

5. Reboot your computer with the bootable diskette and watch the display carefully. One of the early messages that flashes on your

screen will be put there by the new video driver, advising you that it is installed and listing its name and version.

If you follow this procedure carefully, your video system will be up and operating from the A: drive, with the new device driver. Experiment with the CONFIG.SYS file on your bootable diskette until you get the desired results; then copy the new device driver to your hard disk and change the real CONFIG.SYS file (on your hard drive) to call the new device driver.

Software Problems

Problem: My computer is giving me an error message like

Bad or missing filename.SYS
Error in CONFIG.SYS line xx

Solution: Your PC cannot find the file referenced on line xx in your CONFIG.SYS file. It cannot find a driver.

Your hard drive has a file named CONFIG.SYS in the root directory. Examine it for errors; did you just install a new device driver? Make sure you entered its name correctly in the CONFIG.SYS file. And make sure the driver is actually located in the subdirectory you referenced in the file. After all, DOS can't read our minds (which is probably a good thing!).

Problem: I installed some new applications software and now my video display does not work correctly.

Solution: You may need new video driver software.

This is one of the frustrations of upgrading. Remember the diskette that came with your video card? It contained a special device driver for the card. You (or whoever set up your computer) added an entry to your CONFIG.SYS file to use that driver. Now, when you boot your computer, it loads this driver from your CONFIG.SYS file. Look there for an entry such as

    device=C:\VIDEO\MYDRIVER.SYS

This driver may malfunction with your new application software. You may need to contact the company that manufactured your video card, or the retailer where you purchased it. Expect to obtain a diskette with a new version of the device driver software from the company that created the video card, or the one that created the application software.

> **CAUTION**
>
> *Copy your old driver program(s) to a floppy diskette before you install a new one. Keep a copy of the old driver around until you are certain that the new one works well with all your favorite software!*

When you obtain the new driver, look for a program with the same name as the one now referenced in your CONFIG.SYS file. You may need to modify the entry in your CONFIG.SYS file to specify the new driver if the name is even slightly different. After you've made sure that your CONFIG.SYS is correct, copy the new program into the subdirectory where the old one is now located, and then reboot your computer. It automatically uses the newer driver and your video should work just fine!

Problem: My screen has "snow" or a funny, colored border around it.

Solution: DOS is still evolving.

In the course of computer evolution, video hardware first gains features, then the software companies use them. Thus, you may have one application that uses a neat video feature but does not return your display to its original condition on exit. Or you may find a program that leaves your display in a mode another program cannot use.

Consult your application's manual to see if you can change the setup to avoid the problem. Good examples of this are telecommunications programs that let you sacrifice video speed to eliminate video snow. Unfortunately, in some cases you may need to reboot your computer to fix problems of this sort.

In these cases, contact your retailer or the company who made the hardware, to obtain a new software driver. If they cannot assist you, contact the folks who wrote the application to obtain an upgraded version.

Most companies will work to keep you satisfied. If you find one that will not, tell everyone you meet!

Problem: I expected to see a document, but I am only seeing garbage.

Solution #1: You may need to display your file (a letter or whatever) with the application that created it.

Computer files can be stored on your disk in many different formats. Most word processors and spreadsheets store files in their own, unique formats. If you use the DOS TYPE command to view a file created with a word processor, you may see odd characters scroll up your screen, or your computer may beep or act strangely. This does not mean that your file is damaged. It means that you must view and print the file from within the application that created it.

Some applications let you choose the storage format when you SAVE the file. Does yours? This is handy if you wish to move files from one application to another.

Other applications let you specify the file format when you OPEN or begin work on an existing file. The application then translates the file from its original format to one that it can understand. Here's a word of warning: if you use this feature, then resave the file, it probably is saved in the format appropriate to the program that you're now using, not the original format! This could be troublesome if you need to use it again later, with the program that created it.

File format conversions can alter essential aspects of your data. For example, if you use a spreadsheet program to create a monthly sales forecast, then save it only as an ASCII or TEXT file, the file loses the mathematical capability the spreadsheet provided. This is fine if you have a one-time need to include the numbers in a letter to your sales manager, but if you want to use the file again as a spreadsheet, you also should save it in the sheet format, perhaps with a slightly different name.

See Chapter 12, "Problems with DOS and Memory," and Chapter 8, "Problems with Printers and Fonts," for more information about file formats.

Solution #2: You may be using the wrong application or you may need to specify the file's complete name.

This is another of DOS's growing pains. Some applications let you load files created by other programs, and they depend on the filename or its extension to determine the file format. This is fine if the file is named correctly, but many applications let you select both the name and the extension when you SAVE a file. And you always can use DOS to rename a file.

So, if you have trouble viewing a file, refer to your application's manual to see which file formats it can read and what nomenclature it expects. In most cases you'll already have some idea of which program created the file. Don't be afraid to experiment a little bit; that's how we learn!

Solution #3: You may be using the wrong version of the application.

Your file is not necessarily damaged! You may have encountered another of DOS's growing pains. As software improves, it becomes more complex. (Bet you didn't know *that* . . .) Most applications read files generated by their earlier versions, but perhaps not those generated by later versions. This is called *upward compatibility* and is every software manufacturer's headache.

So, if you have trouble viewing a file, refer to your application's manual to see which previous versions it supports and what filename nomenclature it expects. Perhaps you need to use a newer version of the application.

Problem: I expected a different display than I got . . .

Solution: You may need to change your application's setup, or you may need a newer version of the application software.

This diagnosis applies to the number of lines on your display and the background and foreground colors you see. You may find that a particular program "trashes" your display selections. Okay, you bought a fancy new video system. The diagnostics have shown you that it can display 43 lines on your screen. Hot dog! Maybe you used a utility program to set the lines or colors as you wanted them. Then you fired up your word processor and . . . bingo! You got the same old 25-line display, with the same old colors and poor resolution. What happened?

The problem is that your video system is capable of a better display but your application doesn't know it, so it's not using it. Although this situation is improving as DOS matures, in most cases the application program is responsible for your entire visual environment while it has control of your machine. You must tailor each application to your desires.

You may be able to change your application's setup or you may need to reinstall the program. Unfortunately, you may also have to live with the problem until the software manufacturer releases a new version. Be sure to contact them (or your retailer) to see when (or if) they'll be dealing with this growing pain. Did you remember to try this software with this video system before you purchased it?

We covered a lot of territory in this chapter. You learned how to shop for video systems and install their software. Perhaps you even played with your video drivers or diagnostics. You saw that your video system's configuration can be established by your CONFIG.SYS file and you learned how application programs and file formats can affect your display. Now let's move on to some problems with files.

Problems with Files

Using DOS to find lost data is a lot like learning poker. There are a few simple rules you have to learn before it really gets to be fun. In any case, DOS gives you some wildcards to play with, and this book is your ace!

People have come up with many ways to store and move data, some more long-lasting than others. Storage choices seem to depend on ease-of-use, economics, and how long you want to keep the data. Although most files are stored on diskettes or a hard drive, today's computers offer several general choices:

- RAM drives—very fast, dense (compact), reasonably cheap, not very durable

- Hard drives—slower, less dense, more durable, more expensive

- Diskettes —even slower, less dense, less durable, a lot cheaper

- Paper—slowest, least dense, arguably more durable, cheapest

Some people like to use the RAM memory card for laptop computers. These are handy but definitely not cheap; and their durability is questionable because they use tiny batteries that eventually must be replaced.

The newest media are CD ROMs, noted for their high capacity and use of laser optics for reading data. They're very compact and expensive. CDs will be an exciting option when their prices drop to reasonable levels and we can write to them as well as read them.

Consider the media when you store or look for a file. If what you lost was on your hard disk, it's still probably there. If it was on a RAM disk, however, and you turned off the computer or experienced a power failure, it's probably gone; don't even bother to look for it. RAM disks are the most volatile, or easy-to-lose, forms of storage in your PC. Now you see why some folks insist on having an *uninterruptible power supply (UPS)* for their PCs.

When you go looking for a file, you should generally seek it by name, although you also can search by content (what's in the file) or the date or time it was last modified. You even can search for a file of a particular size, in bytes. DOS has simple rules for naming and storing files, much like the "rules" for naming our children.

Rule #1 — Short Is Simple

You'd probably rather name your child Bob than Rufustangaryrobert because it's simpler (among other things). Well, a DOS filename is very simple; it can have only eleven characters, but it can have two parts.

The first part (the actual filename) can be up to eight characters and the second (the extension), only three. (See Table 10.1.) A file must have a first name but the extension is optional.

Table 10.1   Some IBM File Extensions.

File Extension	*File Type*
.BAK	Backup File
.BAS	BASIC Language Program
.BAT	Batch File
.DAT	Data File
.DOC	Document File
.HLP	Help File
.TXT	Text (ASCII) File

Rule #2 — Use the Alphabet

Have you ever met someone named Bob*$%? We don't usually include punctuation in our names, and neither does DOS, but of course there are exceptions to this rule. You may see (or use) occasional embedded characters, such as BOB_1.DOC, but never use spaces in filenames.

Unfortunately, some programs do let you do this, but DOS does not understand it, because DOS uses spaces in an entirely different way.

Rule #3 — Consider Your Ancestors

My last name is Barrett because that was my father's family name. Many children now have last names that are a combination of both parents' family names. DOS has family names too, but we call them *pathnames*. Subdirectories are the "children" of the *root directory*. We even speak of "descending" down into a directory structure, or moving upward to the "parent" directory.

Another common directory structure is the *tree*, which includes a root and *branch directories*. Unfortunately, this analogy is abused; I've seen roots on the left, right, top, and bottom, which makes no sense to me. I know what a tree looks like!

Rule #4 — Consider Your Audience

You may have two friends named Bob. They have different last names, but you probably don't address them so formally unless they're both at your house. Instead, you generally just call them each Bob—DOS works the same way.

You might, for example, create two different files named BOB.DOC in your computer, but they must be in different subdirectories or on different disks. DOS allows this because their full pathnames are different.

Some examples of full pathnames are

C:\WORK\BOB.DOC
C:\FAMILY\BOB.DOC
A:\WORK\BOB.DOC

In this example, if you're in the C:\WORK subdirectory, you can deal with that BOB.DOC directly, but if you're anywhere else, you must tell your PC which of the files named BOB.DOC you wish to deal with. And your DOS commands can affect either or both files, depending upon how you present the command.

Rule #5 — Be Polite

I hate it when someone yells "Hey, you!" because I think it's rude. (Of course I don't mind it when a stranger is telling me to avoid a falling piano!)

DOS gives you a similar opportunity for generality: *wildcards*. These are DOS's way of saying "Hey you!" because wildcards can affect several files at once. There are two DOS wildcard characters, the question mark (?) and the asterisk (*), known as the "splat" character in tech-y slang.

Use the question mark to replace any single filename character in many DOS commands. For example:

c:\>dir bo?.doc

means about the same thing to DOS as

c:\>dir bob.doc

Use an asterisk to replace several filename characters at once in many DOS commands. For instance:

c:\>dir b*.doc

produces about the same results as

c:\>dir bo*.doc

or

c:\>dir bob.doc

Did you catch that weasel word "about"? If you have several files with similar names, a wildcard DIR command lists all of them. For example:

c:\>dir b*.doc

produces a directory listing of

BOB.DOC   3478 5-06-92 10:12p
BUNGIE.DOC 504   4-26-92 12:38a
BABY.DOC   782   7-08-92 9:29p

if you have those files in your subdirectory. DOS lists every file that matches your wildcard specification, in this case, every file that begins with **b** and ends with **.doc**.

There are limits to the wildcard feature, but they're generally sensible. Don't be afraid to use wildcards to help you search for files, but do avoid wildcards when DELeting files; you might lose more than you bargained for! See your DOS manual for a more complete discussion of wildcards.

Enough introduction. Let's examine some problems and solutions.

Problem: My computer seems to have lost its personality; it no longer recognizes my commands. It even asked me for the date and time at boot.

Solution #1: Perhaps you are booting from the wrong drive.

Most PCs have at least one hard drive, usually identified as the C: drive. And they are generally set up to boot from it if there's no diskette in the A: (floppy) drive.

CAUTION

Wildcards are a powerful DOS feature to help you locate and manage files, but they can be dangerous!

Is there a diskette in your A: drive? Perhaps you have not booted your computer from the usual hard drive. Make sure there's no diskette in the A: drive, then reboot your PC.

Solution #2: Perhaps your AUTOEXEC.BAT file was damaged or deleted.

When DOS boots your system, it can tailor your PC to meet your needs automatically by executing this special *batch file* of DOS commands. If DOS finds AUTOEXEC.BAT during boot, it reads the file automatically and follows the commands.

AUTOEXEC means *automatic execution* and BAT means that it's a DOS batch file. This file must be located in the root directory of the drive from which DOS boots. If your AUTOEXEC.BAT file is missing or damaged, your computer lacks the usual PATH, PROMPT, ENVIRONMENT VARIABLES, and TSR programs. Depending on how it was set up, this can leave you with a pretty dull computer.

Use the DOS DIR command to see if you have an AUTOEXEC.BAT file in your root directory. Type **dir** at the DOS prompt and press **Enter**. You should see something like

Volume in drive C is MYDISK
Volume Serial Number is 16BB-A895
Directory of C:
FINANCES <DIR>   07-19-91 9:23p

```
LETTERS <DIR>    07-06-91  2:27p
COMMAND COM 47845 04-09-91  5:00a
AUTOEXEC BAT 1258 06-06-92  9:47p
CONFIG  SYS 1041  04-05-92  7:52p
 03 file(s) 505144 bytes
12019712 bytes free
C:>
```

This system has both an AUTOEXEC.BAT and CONFIG.SYS file in its root directory. If your AUTOEXEC.BAT file is lost or damaged, check with your service personnel or retailer to obtain another copy. Or you can use a word processor to create a new one.

Here's how a typical AUTOEXEC.BAT files looks. You can view yours by using the TYPE command. Type **type autoexec.bat** at the DOS prompt and press **Enter**.

DOS will ignore batch file entries preceded by double-colons. You can use them to include notes in the file. Of course, you could accomplish the same thing by replacing the double-colons with the DOS REM (remark) statement, but I think it's more difficult to read than the colons.

```
:: AUTOEXEC.BAT for my computer
:: Revised -
:: 21 Jun 92 - Created.
```

```
prompt $p$g
path=c:\mouse;c:\utils;c:\dos50;c:\windows;
:: DOS environmental variables
set comspec=c:\dos50\command.com
:: Memory-resident programs
mouse /c2
```

The first entry is just a header for my information, like a diary. DOS ignores it because of the double-colons, but I use it to keep track of changes I make to the file. It really simplifies troubleshooting!

The first entry that DOS reads is the "prompt" specification. It determines the DOS PROMPT we keep mentioning throughout this book. The "pg" instructs DOS to always include the current drive and subdirectory in the prompt. Without this line, the prompt would include only the drive letter, like C:.

The second entry establishes the DOS PATH. This tells DOS where to search for commands you type.

The third entry tells DOS which "command interpreter" program to use, and where it's located on the hard drive.

The fourth and last entry installs a mouse "driver" program on the COM2: serial port.

Although this is a simple example, batch files can be very complex. There's even a very useful DOS "batch file programming language" (explained in your DOS manuals). You should only have one file named AUTOEXEC.BAT in your system, but you can create many other batch files, with any names you wish, to simplify your life.

It's hard to create an AUTOEXEC.BAT file unless you know exactly what commands to put in it, so your best bet is to get a copy from your most recent backup. You do back up your computer regularly, don't you? Or you can contact your local PC user's group for some help in re-creating your file. You may find someone who will do it for free!

Retrieving Files

Problem: My computer is telling me

> **General failure reading drive A**
> **Abort, Retry, Fail?**

Solution: Your disk may be inserted incorrectly or formatted to the wrong density for that drive, or, if it's a fresh diskette, it may not be formatted.

Recheck your diskette to make sure it's in the drive correctly. Is the drive door or lever closed?

Is the diskette formatted properly for that drive? A 360K drive cannot read a 1.2M diskette because its hardware is not that sensitive. Try reading the diskette in the drive that formatted it.

Problem: My computer is telling me

> **File not found — FILENAME.EXT**
> **0 file(s) copied**

Solution: DOS couldn't find the file you named, in the place you gave.

Remember that DOS isn't smart; it always does exactly what you tell it to do. This error doesn't mean your file is lost, so don't panic! Just recheck your typing and consider your basic assumptions. Perhaps you spelled the name incorrectly, or maybe the file isn't where you thought it was. Try using DIR with the * wildcard to look around on your disk. See the next problem/solution.

Problem: I have misplaced a file somewhere on my disk.

Solution #1: You can use the DOS DIR command to locate the file.

As DOS has matured, its commands have gained a lot of power. DOS 1.0 included the DIR command, which was improved in 2.0 and rewritten in 5.0 to provide help, if you ask for it.

To see which version of DOS you're using, type **ver** at the DOS prompt and press **Enter**. You will see a message such as **MS-DOS Version 5.00**.

Use the DOS DIR command to see a listing of all files (and subdirectories) in your current directory. Type **dir** at the DOS prompt and press **Enter**.

If your directory is long, you can show it wide across the screen and force pauses between screens. Type **dir/w/p** at the DOS prompt and press **Enter**.

Or use a DOS wildcard to get a partial listing, as we discussed earlier. This is a *filtering* mechanism. Type **dir b*.doc** at the DOS prompt and press **Enter**.

You also can give a full pathname to see a listing of the files in a different subdirectory than the one you're now in. Type **dir c:\work** at the DOS prompt and press **Enter**. (Of course, you will need to substitute your subdirectory name for "work" in the above example.)

> **TIP**
>
> *If you are using DOS 5.0, you can append a /? to most commands to see a brief listing of helpful information about the command.*

And you can combine these techniques to obtain partial listings of other subdirectories. Type **dir c:\work\b*.doc** at the DOS prompt and press **Enter**, substituting your subdirectory name, as before.

Solution #2: Use the DOS FIND command to search for some specific text in the file.

How to use FIND varies among versions of DOS, so it's best to consult your DOS manual, then play with the command until you feel comfortable. Generally, you type

FIND string FULLPATHNAME

and press **Enter**. In this command, **string** is what you're looking for and **FULLPATHNAME** is the "search path."

The FIND command has a drawback: it may not be able to locate text in a file that's stored in an odd format. Some word processors, for example, store files in protected formats.

Solution #3: You can locate your missing file with an aftermarket utility program.

There are several search programs that are easier to use than the DOS commands. Some are sold directly, some are shareware, and others exist in the public domain. In many cases they have names such as WHEREIS.COM, FIND.COM, or FGREP.COM. Contact your retailer or your local PC user's group for copies of these utilities.

Problem: My diskette has been damaged somehow. It no longer contains my files.

Solution: Did you put it too close to your video monitor?

Diskettes are somewhat durable but they can lose their information in several ways. Never place your diskettes on or around your monitor; it generates strong magnetic fields than can erase your data very quickly.

You also should keep your disks away from heat and dust, and never touch the shiny brown material that shows through the slots in the diskette's dust jacket.

TIP

Be sure to read Chapter 11, "Problems with Viruses," before loading any shareware or public domain programs onto your system.

Moving Files

First, let's look at the differences between copying and moving a file. Copying is a duplication process, like using a copy machine at work. After you COPY a file, it exists in (at least) two places.

On the other hand, when you move a file, DOS does not create a second copy of it. Instead, the existing file is simply put in another location. This is why backing up your data is a duplication process.

To copy a file named MYLETTER.DOC nested in a WORD subdirectory on the C: drive over to the A: drive, type **copy c:\word\Myletter.doc a:** at the DOS prompt and press **Enter**.

Copying or moving a file can be difficult if you don't understand DOS's tools, or if you need to move the file from one deeply nested subdirectory to another.

To make this job easier, there are special programs known as *file maintenance utilities,* which typically offer you a treelike representation of your subdirectories and the files they contain. You can select one or more source files, then select the target or destination directory and perform the move (or copy).

When the DOS developers recognized the popularity of these utilities, they introduced the DOSSHELL.EXE program in DOS 4.0. With DOSSHELL you can move, copy, delete, open, print, rename, change attributes, and view your files. You also can create, delete, and rename subdirectories. When you use DOSSHELL, you gain a nice, graphic interface but you lose speed.

For many people, DOSSHELL is better than "bare" DOS, but it still requires a bit of study, a mouse, and practice for best results.

Problem: I have several copies of a file; which is the latest?

Solution #1: Compare the file's dates and times of last modification.

When you copy a file, the new copy inherits the date and time of the original. Use the DOS DIR command to list both files. Note their size, date, and time of last modification. Usually, the largest file is the latest one because we typically ADD to our files.

You can use DIR and a wildcard to list all the files beginning with the letters "ch"and with the ".doc" extension. Then you can view their size, date and time of last changes. Type **dir ch*.doc** at the DOS prompt and press **Enter**. This works only if they have files with those names!

Unfortunately, this time and date method is only as good as the clock in your PC. Is your clock always correct? If not, the time and date stamps may be wrong, too!

Then too, if you obtain one or both files from another PC, don't assume that its clock is set the same as yours. It may be entirely different!

To check your time, type **time** at the DOS prompt and press **Enter**. You will see a message such as

> **Current time is 10:12:19.99a**
> **Enter new time:**

You either can type the new time and press **Enter**, or just press **Enter**. Check the date in the same way; type it in and **press** Enter at the DOS prompt.

Solution #2: Use the DOS COMP command to compare the files.

All versions of DOS include a COMP command. This command compares two files on a byte-by-byte basis. Unfortunately, it does a poor job of explaining the differences it finds. You can obtain much better aftermarket utility programs that will compare two files and show you their differences in several useful ways.

To use the COMP command, type **COMP** and both filenames, as in the following example:

C:\>COMP FILENAME#1 FILENAME#2 [enter]
Comparing FILENAME#1 and FILENAME#2
Files are different sizes...

Compare more files (Y/N) ?n

C:\>

Here, COMP reported that the two files were different, then asked if we wanted to do another comparison, but we pressed the "n" key to answer "no." (Be sure to substitute the names of your real files for FILENAME#1 and FILENAME#2, above.)

In DOS V5.0 the COMP command is self-prompting. For example, if you simply type **COMP** and press Enter, it will ask you for the name of each file and for any "options" or "filters" to use. To see what filters can be used, type **COMP /?** and press Enter at the DOS prompt. This is the built-in "help" we mentioned earlier.

Solution #3: Take a good hard look at the contents of both files.

This is probably the hardest way to compare two files, but it's often the safest. In many cases, only you know the minute differences that make one file more valuable than the other.

Problem: My computer is reporting

Insufficient disk space
0 File(s) copied

Solution: There's not enough room for the file at the destination.

Your PC is telling you there's "no room at the inn." (You should have made a reservation!) Your file has not been copied, even partially.

If you are at the DOS prompt, use the DIR command to find the size of your file, then do the same thing to see how much room is available in the target subdirectory or diskette.

If you get this message (or a similar one) from within an application, such as your word processor, save your file to a different disk, perhaps a floppy, instead. Saving it to another subdirectory on the same disk does not work. After you have saved the file, do some immediate housekeeping! Some programs may not work reliably when your disk is nearly full!

TIP

Healthy systems have at least 5 percent of their total storage available to you. If you exceed this amount, consider moving some files to diskettes to free up disk space.

Problem: My computer is reporting

Invalid drive specification
0 File(s) copied

Solution: You were copying a file from one drive to another and accidentally typed the wrong letter for a drive.

Maybe you typed **q:** instead of **a:**; they're nearby on the keyboard. Note that no part of your file has been copied to the destination.

Try the command again, with careful attention to how you're setting it up.

Protecting Files

Problem: My computer is reporting

Access denied
0 File(s) copied

Solution: You are trying to overwrite a *read-only* file, and DOS is complaining.

You already have a file by that name at the destination, and it's a read-only file. Every DOS file can be "locked" with the ATTRIB command so that it cannot be deleted or erased. This also means that it cannot be overwritten with another file of the same name.

Remember our friends named BOB, earlier in this chapter? We learned that DOS allows multiple files with the same local name, but not in the same subdirectory. With this method, each of the files has a unique FULL PATHNAME even though their local names are identical.

Use the DOSSHELL program, or any utility that can clear the offending file's read-only attribute, or status; then repeat the command that caused the problem. Here's how you would mark (and unmark) a file for read-only, using the DOS ATTRIB command:

For example, if you have DOS V5.0 and a file named TEXT.DOC, you can "write-protect" it (give it a "read-only" attribute) by typing **ATTRIB +R TEXT.DOC** and pressing **Enter** at the DOS prompt. (Don't worry . . . it's reversible.)

The ATTRIB command does not echo its activity, so it's a good idea to then type **ATTRIB TEXT.DOC** and press **Enter**. Now the ATTRIB command will show you the file's attributes, listed TO THE LEFT OF the filename.

If the file had no attributes set, the space to the left of the filename would be blank. But since you just made it a "read-only" file, you should see an "R" in the space to the left of the filename.

Were you to leave the file write-protected, your word processing application might complain, so to complete this example, you should make the file writeable once more. Type **ATTRIB -R TEXT.DOC** and press **Enter**.

If you have DOS V5.0 you can also type **ATTRIB /?** and press **Enter** to see the DOS HELP SCREEN on the ATTRIB command, or you can refer to your DOS manual.

You might also ask yourself if you really want to lose the data in the other file. Perhaps you should use a different name for the new file?

By the way, DOS will also complain if you try to overwrite hidden or system files.

Problem: I have a file that I never want to lose!

Solution #1: You can make it a read-only file.

When you protect a file in this way, you will not be able to delete or erase the file, but still you could lose it if you reFORMAT the disk.

If the file is really *that* important, you should probably put one copy in a safe place, away from heat, dust, and stray magnetic fields. I keep some diskettes in my safe deposit box, but since the magnetic information inevitably fades with time, I also keep a printed copy of the information whenever possible.

Your PC also offers another way to *write-protect* your data:

Solution #2: You can store it on a write-protected diskette.

First, copy the file to a diskette, then use the DOS COMP command to make sure that it's unchanged (by COMParing it with the original). Now write-protect the diskette and put it in a safe place. See the next section for more information about write-protecting your diskettes.

Deleting Files

Problem: I cannot seem to get rid of a file.

Solution #1: Your diskette may be write-protected.

Your computer hardware provides another way of marking a file read-only: the write-protect tab. Actually, this can be either a notch or a small, sliding tab, depending upon the size of the diskette.

If you are using 5¼ diskettes, they probably have a square notch on one side. If the notch is absent or covered with opaque tape, your computer can read the diskette but it cannot write to it. Some software manufacturers sell their programs on diskettes that have no notch, to protect the software. In a pinch you can cut a similar notch in these diskettes, but it's easy to accidentally damage the magnetic disk beyond repair.

NOTE

All diskettes have a write-protection scheme, but the way it works depends on the size of the diskette.

The smaller, 3½ diskettes have a hole or window that can be closed with a sliding plastic tab. This tab is a newer write-protection scheme and (of course) works differently than the larger diskettes. Here, the hole must be closed to render the diskette writeable. If you can see through the hole, the diskette is write-protected (read-only). Some of these small diskettes have two such holes, one at each corner, but only one of them has the write-protection tab.

If the file you can't get rid of is a read-only or system file, see the discussion for the previous problem, "I have a file I never want to lose."

Solution #2: Is your directory listing out of date?

The DOS DIR command scans your drive each time you invoke it, so the list you see is always up to date. But many people use aftermarket software to navigate around their disks. Some of these programs also rescan the disk every time you call them, others rescan it only at your direction.

This optional rescan speeds up the program's operation but can confuse you if the program's display of your subdirectories and files becomes outdated. For example, you can delete a file with a DOS command, then use the utility program and notice that the deleted file still appears in its listing. The file is no longer there, of course, but the program hasn't realized it because it's using old information. You must force it to rescan your drive.

If you are using an aftermarket utility, check its manual to see how to force a rescan, or if it's even necessary.

Recovering Deleted or Erased Files

Problem: I think I've accidentally erased a file!

Solution: Don't write anything to your disk!

When you DELete or ERAse a file, DOS does not destroy the data immediately. Instead, it simply changes the directory entry to make that disk space available to other data, as the need arises. The change also alerts the DIR command to exclude that filename from subsequent listings.

The key here is to avoid doing anything that will WRITE or SAVE new data to your disk until you've recovered the lost file.

For example, you can safely hunt around with the DOS DIR command but you should avoid rescanning your disk with those aftermarket utilities we discussed earlier in this chapter. They may SAVE a file to your disk, and DOS might give some of the newly released space (containing your data) to that file.

If you have DOS 5.0, you can use the UNDELETE command to restore the lost file. Or you can use any of several aftermarket utilities to do the same thing. The longer you wait before restoring the file, the greater your chances of losing some of the information forever!

If you are running any programs that periodically save information to your disk, disable them immediately! If you don't know how to disable them, shut your system down in the usual way, then reboot it from a bootable floppy diskette that does not contain the offending program. Now you can examine your hard drive at your leisure.

In general, if you cannot UNERASE the lost file immediately, rebooting from a floppy is the best way to ensure that nothing else is written to your hard drive until you have restored the lost file.

Well, now you know a little bit about DOS file conventions and you've learned some of the ways to protect your data, move it around, and restore it. Now let's discuss a very modern phenomenon: viruses!

Problems with Viruses

By now you've probably heard of viruses, and you may be wondering "What's the big deal?" Well, they are a big deal. According to McAfee Associates, creators of virus checking and removing programs, there were 586 known viruses as of May 21, 1992. If you include the variants of these, the number jumps to 1,302. And, sad though it may be, this number is increasing every day.

This chapter gives you a quick rundown on viruses, what they are, how to detect them, avoid them, and eliminate them.

What Is a Virus?

A virus is a small, hidden program—a hitchhiker. You don't realize it's there until it does whatever it was written to do before you can stop it. Viruses travel by attaching themselves to other programs or data files, or by locating themselves in important parts of your computer, where they can hitch a ride in out-of-the-way places on any diskettes you use.

When you execute an infected program, or open an infected data file, you may also trigger the virus program. It may not cause you trouble immediately. Instead, it may just infect your system. But it will do something unpleasant eventually, and in the meantime, it may be infecting every diskette you put into your computer! Viruses are so named because they can duplicate themselves, just as in the biological world. Some viruses have been known to clog disks with their spawn!

Viruses are such a threat that some software companies market special "immunization" software, which we discuss later in this chapter.

How Do Viruses Travel?

Viruses travel in a wide variety of ways, all of which involve sharing information with other computers. If you never use a modem to transfer a file and never put a diskette from someone else's system in your PC, you won't catch a virus. But you won't have much fun or use of your computer, either.

You may be thinking that if you pay money for the software, through formal retail channels, you'll be safe, right? Nope. Viruses have even been found in expensive software sold by nationwide manufacturers! And one major manufacturer of computers recently found out, much to its chagrin, that it had been shipping computers that had a virus-infected version of DOS loaded on the hard disks.

Many viruses can destroy your data, reformat your hard drive, or lock up your system. Most immunization software includes a complete list of the viruses they detect and their possible effects. The following are just a few of the problems you might encounter; this list is presented only to give you an idea of the diversity of viruses.

- Files seem to be getting bigger all by themselves.
- Files disappear mysteriously.
- The characters on the display fall to the bottom of the screen.
- A "smiley face" appears and eats all the zeros on the screen.
- Programs will not run properly; they crash in odd ways.
- Messages appear on the screen.
- The system acts sluggish and the display flickers oddly.
- The computer unexpectedly plays "Yankee Doodle"!
- There's a "bouncing dot" or "ball" on the display.
- The computer won't boot from the hard disk.

Problem: How can I avoid virus infection?

Solution #1: The best way is to practice what is called safe computing.

Never use any software that you did not remove the shrinkwrap from. Never loan any of your disks to anyone. Keep your computer, and all of its data in an isolation ward. Throw away your modem. (For many of us, this translates into: "Stop having fun.")

Solution #2: Invest in virus protection software, and use it.

There are several very good software packages available. Each of them provides a great measure of protection against virus infection, if it is used properly.

Solution #3: Keep multiple backups of your system.

Backups are very useful. If all your data is erased or garbled by a virus infection, or by a strong magnet for that matter, restore your data from a set of backup disks that you know are uninfected.

Problem: My computer is acting real funny.

Solution: It may be caused by a virus. Don't let all the talk about viruses scare you too much. Infection is still rare, but its risk is growing. See solutions 1, 2, and 3 above.

Curing Viruses

Now you know what they are, how they travel, and what they can do. How can you eliminate one if you have it? Simple! Use immunization software.

Any virus can be detected if you know what to look for, and the folks who write this software make it their business to know. Immunization software automatically compares every file in your system to a master list of virus "signatures"—the clues by which they detect these nasty critters—and warns you when it finds a match. If you are warned, you also are offered a menu of choices, depending upon the severity of the infection. It's a good feeling.

You should obtain and use a virus protection package. It will include several programs to do specific things, such as disinfect your hard drive, inspect diskettes as you use them, and even warn you whenever a program tries to write anything to your disk.

These packages offer various levels of protection, which you can tailor to your needs. For example, you may tire of the warnings each time something is written to your disk, but you can disable that feature without sacrificing the inspection of each new diskette. And you can re-enable the features anytime you wish.

The updates may be free or you may need to subscribe to an update service for a nominal fee. (The company wants to keep you as a customer!)

There is more technical stuff you could learn about viruses, but right now you know enough—what they are, how they travel, some of the things they do, and how to avoid them. Let's go on and talk about memory problems.

Problems with DOS and Memory

In this chapter we discuss how DOS uses memory and the different kinds of memory in your PC. We also explore why the different kinds of memory are necessary, how to tell how much you've got, and how to tell which kind you've got. And you will see what to do when your system's memory is not working correctly. But first, let's look at some common DOS problems.

Booting: The Most Common DOS Problem

Problem: My computer is telling me to

Insert disk with COMMAND.COM in drive A
Press any key to continue

Solution: You need a bootable diskette in drive A:.

This situation can occur when you boot to the A: drive and subsequently change diskettes. If the new diskette is not also bootable, your computer is unable to reload COMMAND.COM (the command interpreter, an essential disk file that must be present for DOS to run) when it needs it. You need to put a bootable diskette in the drive.

This situation can also occur if COMMAND.COM is erased accidentally from your bootable diskette or your hard drive. For now, insert a different, bootable diskette in the A: drive, then copy COMMAND.COM onto the damaged one. Make sure all your disks and diskettes use the same version of COMMAND.COM.

Note that this error message is misleading because bootable disks contain more than just COMMAND.COM; they also include two hidden system files you may never see in your directory. When you use the FORMAT command with the /S switch to create a bootable disk, DOS copies these two hidden files onto a special place on the disk.

TIP

Simply copying COMMAND.COM to a disk or diskette does not make it bootable! You either must format your disk with the /S option or use the DOS SYS command to copy the necessary files.

Problem: My computer is telling me

Bad or missing Command Interpreter

Solution: You need to use a bootable diskette or unlatch your A: drive.

Is the latch on your A: drive closed? If you are attempting to boot to your hard drive, you need to open the latch. If you wish to boot to the A: drive, you must use a bootable diskette.

Problem: My computer is telling me

Invalid media or Track 0 bad - disk unusable
Format terminated

Solution: This disk cannot be made bootable!

A bootable diskette must contain the COMMAND.COM program and two special, hidden files (transferred with the FORMAT command's /S option). The two files must be located in a special place on the disk or diskette: track #0. (Why programmers always begin with zero is lost in ancient scripture, so we just have to take it on faith.)

If the first track (yes, track #0) on a disk is damaged, the disk never can be made bootable, although you may be able to format it as a nonbootable diskette for data storage.

See Chapter 4, "Problems with Disks and Disk Drives," or your DOS manual for more information about bootable disks.

Now that you know that DOS is composed primarily of three files, and that you cannot even see two of them, let's look at the way DOS uses your computer's memory. We have more to say about DOS and command interpreters as we move through the chapter.

Problem: RAM, ROM—extended and expanded—why are there so many kinds of memory?

Solution: Actually, there are only a couple of kinds of memory hardware.

The names you've heard, like extended and expanded, refer to the way memory is wired (or configured) in your system.

Your RAM, or Read Only Memory, is the workhorse memory hardware in your computer. When you boot your PC, it loads a copy of the DOS command interpreter (COMMAND.COM) into a special place in RAM, then executes that copy. When you run an application program, the PC copies it into memory and executes it.

Even your data is often stored temporarily in RAM before it's given a more permanent home, such as a file on your hard drive. When you SAVE a file, you are copying it from RAM to your disk. So, it's a good idea to frequently SAVE your data files as you're working.

As application software has evolved, it has required ever larger amounts of RAM memory, so today's computers can use a lot more memory than ones just a few years old. The first IBM PC could address a whopping 1M of RAM, but only 16K was installed. The designers had planned ahead and allowed room for a total of 640K of RAM (ten times the original amount!), but they only installed 16K because memory chips were very expensive and 16K was sufficient to run the biggest programs they'd seen.

Almost as soon as the PC was introduced, folks were complaining that they needed more memory. Finally, a group of manufacturers conceived expanded memory.

Expanded memory is somewhat slow to access, and it has other problems, too. You can't actually run a program in expanded memory; it only holds data or inactive programs. But it was much faster than disk storage, and it was the only alternative, so everyone considered it worthwhile. Soon many programs required this new memory and would not function properly without it. Unfortunately, expanded memory required a software driver that also used up some conventional (640K) memory space.

The next major change occurred when IBM introduced a machine with a new microprocessor. The PC-AT computers used an Intel 80286 chip, which "extended" the possible memory space, but you still had to install RAM chips. And of course, you still could add expanded memory of several megabytes for the programs that required it.

Today's PCs generally use newer 386 or 486 microprocessors, and the 80586 is rapidly becoming available. You can install extended memory and you also can add expanded memory if you wish. Most folks avoid expanded memory now because it's slow, but some programs still require it and most computers let you set up a portion of your extended RAM as expanded memory. Whew! Wouldn't it be nice if we could dispense with these concerns about memory and just use the darn computers?

How Much Memory Do You Need?

Your computer's memory requirements vary with the combination of programs you use and the way you use them. See Figure 12.1. You need enough memory to run your programs as fast as you wish and as many as you wish at once (but there are limits on this). Before we discuss this in detail, we need to refresh *our* memory about memory-resident programs.

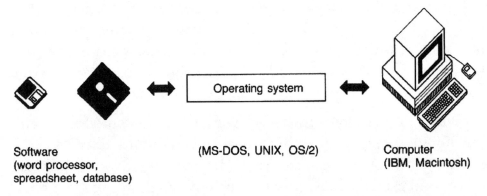

Software
(word processor,
spreadsheet, database)

(MS-DOS, UNIX, OS/2)

Computer
(IBM, Macintosh)

Figure 12.1 Operating systems control hardware resources, such as memory, CPU time, and disk space.

Most of your application programs occupy only conventional memory while they are running. When you quit, they release the memory for other uses. On the other hand, memory-resident programs occupy memory until you reboot your computer (or deinstall them). In fact, they are always running, although you may not be using them at the moment.

If you install several memory-resident programs, they each use up some of your conventional memory and you may not be able to execute large applications. Until recently, your only choice was to limit their use or install other special programs to swap them in and out as you needed them. DOS 5.0 lets you locate your memory-resident programs in other areas of memory so that they don't use up your conventional memory.

This is by no means a complete discussion of memory-resident programs. We have not touched on their tendency to assume control of parts of your computer, because it's a complicated subject. All you really need to know is that they can conflict with each other and the best way to learn about them is to experiment. Some must be the first program you install, others must be the last. Some will just not work well with others and some will conflict with your applications.

If you think you have conflicts among your memory-resident programs, run them one at a time. If they each function properly, then run them two at a time, and so forth. If this exacting drudgery bores you to tears, use a different program or contact your local PC users group for advice.

Problem: My application aborted with an "out of memory" error, or words to that effect.

Solution #1: You may need to free up some conventional memory.

Conventional memory is the 640K memory we discussed earlier. It has a fixed size, and most programs use a bit of it. If you have several memory-resident programs installed, there may not be enough space left for your application.

Look in the manual that came with your application to establish its memory requirements; then try rebooting with no memory-resident programs to see if the application runs properly. If it does, you need to decide which memory-resident programs you can do without.

The quickest way to do this test is to boot your PC from a bootable diskette in the A: drive. Make sure the diskette contains no AUTOEXEC.BAT or CONFIG.SYS files. After you've booted in this way, change to the directory where your application is located and run it as usual.

If you are using DOS 5.0, you may be able to load your memory-resident programs into *high memory*. This releases more memory for your applications. See the LOADHIGH command in your DOS manual.

Solution #2: You may need to exit your present command interpreter.

Some programs let you temporarily *push* or *shell out* or switch back to DOS. When you do this, you will see a message advising you to

Type EXIT to return to DOS

This is a convenient way to put your application on hold, but you pay a memory penalty. When you "push to DOS," you start another copy of the DOS command interpreter program, COMMAND.COM. While it's running, your original computing environment is stored in RAM temporarily, waiting for your return. In this situation you may not have enough free memory to do much except see directory listings. You may not even be able to print a file! In extreme cases, you won't be able to shell out because the computer has no room to run another copy of the command interpreter.

If you shell out and try to rerun your application, you may get an "out of memory" message. Just type **exit** at the DOS prompt and press **Enter** to regain your former environment.

Actually, shelling out is a bad habit because you may forget you did it and begin editing the same file all over again. When you subsequently return, you could lose your latest work!

Problem: My program is running much slower than I expected.

Solution: It may not have access to the kind of memory it needs.

Some application programs can use extended or expanded memory to speed up their operation, if it's available. If you install these programs incorrectly or if your computer is not set up to make the memory available, the program will not run at its best.

Read the manual that came with the program to see if you could benefit by installing it differently or making more (or different) memory available, and then experiment with your computer's setup. After all, you can't hurt it.

TIP

*Always make a
backup copy of your
AUTOEXEC.BAT or
CONFIG.SYS files before
changing them. Then, you can
quickly revert to them if
your experiments
are not
fruitful.*

Problem: I set up my PC properly, but my program still runs slowly.

Solution #1: Some other program may be hogging your memory.

Extended and expanded memory typically involve memory manager or driver programs. These two types of system software are usually installed at boot.

Some applications will work with these drivers but others need raw, unmanaged memory. Be sure that your application and your drivers are working in concert, not in conflict. For example, your memory manager may have "claimed" all your extended memory at boot. If your application needs unclaimed extended memory, none will be available. See the discussion of the DOS MEM command later in this chapter, then learn how to install your memory manager to leave some free memory for your application.

Solution #2: Your computer may be running much slower than necessary.

Some computers can operate at various speeds. If your computer has a turbo switch or mode, activate it, then try running the application again. It may make no difference, but you won't know until you try!

Some serial ports malfunction if the computer is run at high speed. You may need to slow these machines when you run a telecommunications program, for example, then speed them up again for word processing or spreadsheet applications. You may be able to create a batch file that will do this for you automatically.

CAUTION

Always save your data before changing your computer's speed!

TIP

Batch files are handy for tailoring your system to run programs in special ways.

Problem: I cannot run the same application I used a while ago.

Solution: You may have less memory available now.

Did you install a memory-resident program in the meantime? Some programs become memory-resident when you least expect it. For example, the first time you PRINT a file after booting, the PRINT.EXE program becomes resident. If you boot, run a program, and print something, and then find that you cannot run the same program again, it may be because PRINT is taking up some of your conventional memory.

If you have a recent version of DOS, you can use the MEM command with a special switch to see which programs are resident right now. The MEM command varies with your version of DOS, so refer to your DOS manual for information about the available switches. Look for one like /PROGRAM. You type **mem/program** and press **Enter.**

How Much Memory Do You Have?

You usually can see how much memory you have when your computer boots. Watch the display for a counter that ticks by rapidly. If your computer has a turbo mode, you can slow the counter by slowing the computer; just turn off the turbo mode . . . but remember to turn it back on later!

When you see this counter, it means that your computer is locating and testing its RAM memory. The count is usually expressed in kilobytes (K), so a number such as (**4194**) indicates that your computer has at least 4,194,304 bytes, or 4M of memory. The next section shows you another way to find out more about your computer's memory.

How Is Your Memory Being Used?

You see how much memory you have and how it's organized with the DOS MEM command. Just type **mem** at the DOS prompt and press **Enter**. Depending on your version of DOS, you should get a display similar to

> **655360 bytes total conventional memory**
> **655360 bytes available to MS-DOS**
> **572800 largest executable program size**
> **3407872 bytes total contiguous extended memory**

> **0 bytes available contiguous extended memory**
> **3325952 bytes available XMS memory**
> **C:\>**

Of course, your numbers may be different, but let's examine these for practice. Notice that 640K is a shorthand way of saying 655,360 bytes, or about .6M.

In this example, the PC has a full complement of conventional memory, but only 572,800 bytes are available because the rest is in use by the DOS system, various software drivers, and memory-resident programs. The largest application you could run would be one requiring 572,800 bytes of conventional memory.

Do you see that it has assigned 3,407,872 bytes of memory for use as extended memory? This extended memory is evidently controlled by a memory manager program, so none is directly available. Your programs must request it from the memory manager.

Don't worry if the numbers we've used here don't make a lot of sense to you at first. Folks typically do a lot of rounding off when discussing memory. If you wish, you can review the explanation of binary arithmetic in a more technical PC book.

The point of all this is that the MEM command is very useful. You can use it to see how much memory your programs are using and how your memory is allocated to various uses. If you have a newer version of DOS, the MEM command is even more useful because it also shows you which programs are occupying which areas in memory. See your DOS manual for more information.

If you just don't like the MEM command, there are many good utility programs that show you the same information in other ways. Ask your friends, your retailer, and your local PC users group for their opinions. I can guarantee you'll get an earful!

In this chapter you learned how DOS uses your memory and why there are several types of memory. We introduced the MEM command and showed you how it can help you understand your memory configuration. Now let's examine things from a different angle and discuss some general problems you may encounter with software.

Problems with Software

Computers are a lot like an orchestra. When everything is working in harmony, the melodies are truly beautiful. But a poor arrangement or an off-key instrument, or even a musician having a bad night can spoil the whole performance. Computers, like orchestras, are composed of many parts which must work together for the best effect. This is the chapter where we examine the quality of the music our computers are making!

In earlier chapters we discussed the various components of your computer's orchestra: cables, printers, memory, video, and other hardware; drivers, files, and other software. Now that we've met the orchestra and reviewed the score, let's look at some sour notes that could keep you from computing beautiful music.

Installation Problems

Most software manufacturers spend lots of effort to make software installation simple. Figure 13.1 shows you some typical pieces of a software kit. A difficult installation can kill an otherwise promising product. Installation may be as simple as copying everything from the diskette(s) to your hard disk, or you may need to run a special installation program or batch file included on one of the diskettes.

Some programs are not meant to be installed; you simply place the diskette in your drive, close the drive's latch, and run the program from the original diskette.

In most cases, the manufacturer includes some kind of instructions, either as a manual, a leaflet, or a sentence printed on the disk label. If you find absolutely no instructions, contact the retailer where you purchased the software. This need for instructions and possible assistance is a good reason to purchase software instead of using "pirated" copies of popular programs.

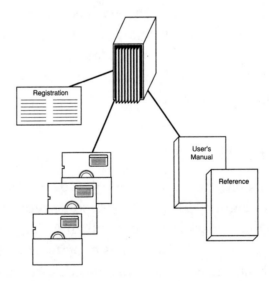

Figure 13.1 Typical software kit.

Problem: I've never installed anything. Where do I begin?

Solution: Use common sense and follow a few simple steps.

When you purchase software, you usually receive some distribution diskettes, one or more manuals, and a warranty card. You also may receive several smaller books or leaflets with names such as "Installation Guide," "Quick Install," or "Read Me First." If you received an instruction manual, look in the Table of Contents for a section about installation, and begin there.

Most software includes one or more special *Readme* files on the installation diskette (sometimes identified as the Install disk, Diskette #1, or the Program disk). This text file probably is named README, README.TXT, NEWS.DOC, or something similar. You can use the DOS DIRectory command to examine each disk for such files. Just put each disk in your disk drive, type **dir a:** at the DOS prompt, and press **Enter**.

TIP

If you use "pirated" software, you don't have access to the help and expertise you may need. It also violates copyright laws.

TIP

Handle your distribution diskettes carefully! Make copies of the original disks; then store the originals safely away and install the software from the copies.

When you do this, you should see the disk's directory listing (a list of all files on the disk) scroll across your screen. If your diskette is in your B: drive, substitute **b:** for the **a:** in the example.

Readme files usually are stored in an ASCII text format you can read with the DOS TYPE command. For example, to view a file named README.DOC located on a diskette in your A: drive, type

> **type a:readme.doc**

and press **Enter**. The contents of the file will scroll across your screen so that you can read it. If the file scrolls too fast for easy reading, you can print it with the DOS PRINT command and then read it at your leisure. Type

> **print a: readme.doc**

and press **Enter**. Of course, if your Readme file has a different name, substitute that name for the words **readme.doc**.

You should always look for such files before beginning an installation because they are your very latest source of information about the product. For example, they may alert you to errors or omissions in the manual!

Some manufacturers give you a special program with which to see the Readme file. It works like the TYPE command but gives you more control over the display. If you see a file named READ.EXE or README.EXE, it may be for this purpose.

Regardless of the method, you should print the text files and keep them handy for a few days, until you're sure the software is working properly.

Problem: I installed some software, then lost it!

Solution #1: It's probably still there; try reinstalling it.

Most software installation programs will not harm existing data that's on your disk, but they often do generate new subdirectories. If you reinstall a software package, it may ask you questions that remind you where you installed it. Or it may perform a much shortened version of the original installation, once it locates the earlier copy.

In any event, once you locate it again, write down the full pathname of its location, and jot down some notes to remind yourself how to run the application—perhaps in the margins of the instruction manual.

TIP

Always look for Readme files when you receive new software. They're usually stored in ASCII text format and can be read with the DOS TYPE command.

Solution #2: How are you seeking it?

Many folks use aftermarket utility programs to navigate around their hard disks. These programs present you with a treelike display of your subdirectories, and you use the arrow keys or a mouse to select your destination. These are very useful utilities, but they have a drawback: they are not continually in contact with DOS, so their displays can become outdated.

When you install software, it may create new subdirectories on your disk, but it probably won't tell the navigational utility program about them. You must "force" the utility to update its tree-picture; then you will see the new subdirectories. This same problem can occur if you delete a subdirectory; the display still may indicate that it exists. See your utilities manual for directions on updating its display.

Solution #3: Accept the default answers during the first installation.

This is a problem with anything new; if we knew all about it, it wouldn't be new. Many installation programs and batch files ask questions that make sense to the manufacturer but less sense to us, the neophytes. One hopes that in time they will learn to put themselves in our shoes, but I wouldn't bet the farm on it.

These installation programs also typically offer a simplifying option, whether it's a preselected menu item or an "easy installation." Just bear in mind that it's only software! If you're unhappy with the initial installation, you can always go back and change it later.

There are some sensible precautions you can take to make life easier, such as backing up important files before attempting the installation. That way, if something goes wrong you haven't lost anything and you can restore your preinstallation environment quickly while you place that call to your retailer!

Problem: I installed some software, then forgot how to run it.

Solution #1: Look in the manual.

Most software comes with instructions that explain how to install it, configure it, and operate it. I know it's boring, but you really should become familiar with your manuals. Look for chapters with titles like "Running the Application" or "Start-Up."

Solution #2: Perhaps you must configure it for your needs.

TIP

Back up your data, AUTOEXEC.BAT, and CONFIG.SYS files before installing new software. Then if the installation fails, you can restore your system quickly.

Installation programs have one major purpose: to get the software onto your disk. When that is done, some installers configure it for you automatically, others remind you to do it, and still others just exit to DOS or start the application.

Sit back for a moment and consider your entire system. Ask yourself what hardware this application uses. For example, does it require a mouse? Where is yours connected? COM1? COM2? *Is* it connected? Does this new application know that? As always, check your manual.

Solution #3: Are you executing it from the correct subdirectory?

Some software should be executed only from the subdirectory where it's installed. Other programs are intended to be run from anywhere in your system. This fundamental choice can be confusing because it involves additional work during setup. Making software run from anywhere within your system is a bit more complicated than making it run "locally."

If your new application is in your DOS PATH, you can call it from anywhere within your system. If it's not in your path, you need to change to its subdirectory in order to run it. See the next problem/solution for more information.

Problem: I installed the software but it won't run properly.

Solution: Perhaps you must configure your system a bit more.

At boot, your computer may use an AUTOEXEC.BAT file to establish your DOS PATH. When you type a command on your keyboard, DOS searches the PATH for that command. Perhaps your PATH needs to be modified for this new software?

Some installation programs are very selfish. They revise the PATH in your AUTOEXEC.BAT file to point only to their new subdirectories! Other installers politely add their subdirectories to your existing PATH. And of course, some let you (or make you) modify the PATH statement yourself.

Your AUTOEXEC.BAT file may also contain a DOS APPEND statement, which is like a PATH to your data files. If it is incorrect or missing, your application may not be able to locate its data files or configuration information.

Software installation also can require new DOS environment variables for your system. Environment variables, or ENVARS, are like a receptionist's In/Out board: they tell your applications where to find necessary resources.

In general, software installation can involve any of the following steps:

● Creating one or more new subdirectories

● Copying the software to your disk

- Revising the drivers specified in your CONFIG.SYS file
- Revising the PATH statement in your AUTOEXEC.BAT file
- Revising the APPEND statement in your AUTOEXEC.BAT file
- Revising the ENVIRONMENT VARIABLES in your AUTOEXEC.BAT file
- Rebooting your system to let these changes take effect

Of course, very few installations need to change all of these, but any of them could be affected. A good installer program does these things for you, but none are perfect because the computers are all so different. Some folks don't want an installer to reboot their system, yet it may be necessary. You always should check your instructions to learn what must be done and ensure that each step is performed correctly.

Operation Problems

Assuming that your software is correctly installed, most of the operating problems you may encounter will be caused by poorly written applications, your lack of experience, or conflicts among your various applications. After you install a new application, it's a good idea to test your other applications, to uncover potential conflicts early in the game.

Problem: How do I start my new application?

Solution: Look for an executable program or a batch file.

Application programs always start in one of two ways. In some cases, you must type their name; in others you type the name of a DOS batch file that calls the application, as if you had typed its name.

Recall that there are several kinds of files in your computer but only two types are executable programs. You can recognize these in a directory listing because their names end with either .COM (a command file) or .EXE (an executable command file).

The DOS rules of the road are that you can run any executable program by typing its name at the DOS prompt. For example, to PRINT a file, you run the PRINT.EXE program by typing

PRINT filename

and pressing **Enter.** Be sure to substitute your file's actual name for **filename** in the above example.

The other way to start an application is to run a DOS batch file, a file ending with the .BAT extension. Remember, a batch file is an ASCII text file that contains one or more DOS commands, one per line. When you run the batch file, your computer acts as if you had entered each command from the DOS prompt. Batch files are a convenient way to group a series of DOS commands together so that you don't need to remember them. For example, your application may provide a batch file that installs a memory-resident driver it needs and then starts the application. When you later exit the application, the batch file may remove the memory-resident program from your memory. (Or it may not, in which case you will not have access to that memory until you reboot your computer. This would be an example of a poorly written batch file.)

The instruction manuals that came with your application should tell you about any included batch files. And you can use EDLIN, EDIT (DOS 5.0), or your favorite word processor to create your own batch files.

Problem: My application worked fine yesterday, but it won't run today.

Solution #1: Review the other things you've done since yesterday.

We began this chapter with a comparison to an orchestra: everything must work in harmony. Did you change your system or install another program yesterday? Perhaps that created a conflict with this application?

Solution #2: You may need to reboot your computer.

It's always a good idea to see if rebooting solves a problem. If so, then there's another, bigger problem, but you may not need to fix it today. Just make a note of the circumstances and then get on with today's work.

Some programs are poor housekeepers; when they quit or exit, they don't leave things in your computer as they found them. Be alert for programs of this type, report this behavior to the software manufacturer, and expect them to take such reports seriously. You may find that they are already aware of it and can tell you how to work around the bug until a new version is released.

Some PCs are very sensitive to AC power-line disturbances. These electrical storms can confuse the computer or upset something in its memory. In the worst cases, they even can damage your computer permanently! If you must live with "dirty power," consider using a surge protector or an uninterruptable power supply. Discuss the problem with your power company and see your retailer for more information.

Problem: My computer is reporting that it's "out of memory" or has "insufficient memory."

Solution: You may be running too many programs at once.

Each program requires some memory space in which to run. It's easy to install so many memory-resident programs that a large application will have insufficient memory in which to operate. Review Chapter 12, "Problems with DOS and Memory," and then see how your memory is being used. Did you just run an application that installed a memory-resident program, but neglected to remove it later?

Problem: My application program just bombed or returned to DOS unexpectedly.

Solution: You did not do anything wrong; you may have found a bug!

Programs should never quit unexpectedly, but they sometimes do! Unfortunately, we just have to live with this possibility, but help is always available. If this happens to you, write down a detailed list of your equipment and what you were doing when the program bombed. Check your manual for a section that lists the possible error messages and see if yours is included; then contact the software manufacturer. They may already be aware of the bug. And they may be able to send you a corrected version of the program.

Upgrade Problems

Consider why you would install a software upgrade. Either the present version is buggy or you want the additional features in the new version. Either way, you are changing the way your system will work, so it's a lot like a new beginning.

Problem: What's the safest way to upgrade a system?

Solution: Assume that it may cause problems and protect yourself!

TIP

SAVE your work frequently if you are having problems of any kind! A little extra effort here can keep you from losing valuable data!

You should always back up your system before beginning an upgrade. The extent of the backup depends on how difficult it would be for you to reinstall your system and restore your data if it were lost or damaged.

For example, if you are upgrading your favorite word processor, you should at least copy all your document files onto diskettes, for safety. You might also copy everything in the subdirectory to another subdirectory, perhaps named TEMP. Then if the upgrade is successful, you can go back and delete the TEMP subdirectory.

If you are upgrading your operating system—perhaps moving to a new version of DOS—you have a much larger task. You should copy your data files and documents as a matter of course. You also should make copies of your AUTOEXEC.BAT and CONFIG.SYS files, in case you need to revert to your present version of DOS. I don't like waiting for files to be copied to diskettes, so I usually copy my entire DOS system into an out-of-the-way subdirectory named TEMP, and then handle it as mentioned earlier.

Problem: The upgrade has a different installation procedure.

Solution: Yup. This can happen.

Unfortunately, upgrading is not always as simple as copying everything onto your hard drive. Your best approach is to treat the upgrade as a new software package: back up your present software, read the manuals, and look for Readme files on the new diskettes before doing anything else.

Problem: The upgrade seems incomplete.

Solution: You may be installing a partial upgrade.

Some software companies include in upgrades only those programs which have changed; others send you a completely new package. The partial upgrades are less expensive, but you must pay very close attention to the instructions or you may have problems! Partial upgrades are growing in popularity because distribution diskettes and manuals are expensive to produce. Partial upgrades offer you improved applications for a lower cost.

Problem: My freshly upgraded system is not working correctly.

Solution: The upgrade may be buggy or it may not work on your system.

If an upgrade is released to correct major software bugs, it implies a lot of pressure and a flurry of activity by the programmers, so other odd bugs may creep into the software. Essentially, they fix one thing and break several others.

Just delete the upgraded software and restore or reinstall your original version; then call your retailer or the manufacturer. You did back up your original installation before beginning the upgrade, didn't you?

Upgrades may no longer work with other parts of your system. For example, the new software may no longer support your old printer. You may need to use one or more files from the earlier system. A good example of this is a note you can find in the DOS 5.0 manual. It discusses a program named HIMEM.SYS that is included with both DOS 5.0 and Windows 3.0. It advises you that the two programs are different, although they have the same name (!) and directs you to use the one that comes with DOS 5.0 if you are running Windows 3.0. This sort of thing can be confusing, so proceed carefully!

TIP

Always back up your software before attempting an upgrade. Better safe than sorry!

Version Control Problems

OK, you upgraded your software and everything seemed fine at the time, but now you've got some strange problems. What's going on?

Problem: The new version of my application won't read older data files.

Solution: The new version may not be able to read older data files directly, but it will maintain upward compatibility somehow.

Most new versions of any software maintain upward compatibility with data files or documents generated by earlier versions. This is one of the software manufacturer's unavoidable responsibilities.

If this happens to you, review your manual for a way to update your older files. Most companies recognize this requirement and give you some way to proceed. Look for keywords such as "import," "update," or "modify." Be alert for weasel words that mean that you will lose some information or formatting. You may need to keep a copy of the older version of the application around until the old data files are outdated.

If all else fails, call the manufacturer for assistance. There have been cases in which customers sent copies of data files to manufacturers for upgrading.

Problem: The new version of my application won't print correctly.

Solution: You may need to install a different printer driver.

Printers are changing very fast. Their new abilities can cause problems with older software. When a manufacturer releases an upgraded software package, it may include new drivers, which may work differently than you'd expect. Or they may have slightly different names.

Review your software's setup to see how to specify the driver for your printer. You may need to reconfigure your application or revise your CONFIG.SYS file slightly.

Problem: The new version of my application does funny things to my video display.

Solution: You may need to install revised video driver software.

Application upgrades often include new video drivers. You may need to choose between the driver that came with the new software and the one that you received with your video system. Do you recall installing a special driver when you purchased the video system? Those folks know more about their hardware than the people who wrote the application software, so you may want to modify your CONFIG.SYS file to use the older driver.

Contact your retailer or the company that manufactured the video board. They may be able to provide a new driver for your new application. This is good advice for problems you encounter with any of your peripherals during an upgrade.

In this chapter we listened to the whole orchestra! We looked at how your entire system performs with your software applications. We discussed installing them, using them, and upgrading them. You learned that each step can present different problems, but that there are always solutions. You saw that you should keep the general flow of your system in mind when considering a problem, and that, in many cases, there is more than one way to proceed—but there's usually one that is easier or cheaper or quicker.

Preventative Maintenance

You might very well be asking yourself, "Maintenance? What can go wrong with a computer? It's electronic! Nothing moves!" And you're partially correct; computers are electronic but they are also mechanical, and those parts definitely benefit from some routine housekeeping. After all, you may have paid several thousand dollars for your system, so why not give it a little TLC every so often?

Besides, we're talking *preventative* maintenance here, the kind that you do instead of waiting until it breaks down. This maintenance also includes data maintenance—ensuring that your files are available when you need them, not accidentally changed or destroyed.

Maintaining a Log

If you've read through this book, you've seen that computers are complex combinations of some very simple parts. More troubles occur because of the way the parts are organized than because of the parts themselves! For example, if your co-worker or a family member makes a simple change to your PC's configuration, you may spend the rest of the day wondering what's wrong with it. This actually is more of a communication problem than a computer problem, but there are at least two ways to solve it.

First, if more than one person uses the PC, consider hanging a *logbook* next to it. Then, whenever anyone has a problem or installs new software or changes the machine's setup, encourage that person to make a short entry in the logbook. A two-minute entry can save hours of troubleshooting.

In the best world, you would keep this log file in the computer, but not everyone uses the same word processor and a real book hanging nearby seems to be more noticeable. Also, you need the file if the computer breaks, and that's the one time it would not be available if it's stored on disk! If you are the only one who uses the PC, you still should keep records for review, like a diary, for the same reasons.

This next suggestion is highly tech-y, and I apologize. If several folks use the computer, perhaps you can assign one person to be the *system administrator* or *system operator.* Let that person make any changes, install software upgrades, and generally care for the system. The administrator should also maintain the logbook, although everyone should use it. And consider rotating the "SYSOP" responsibility every month or so, to ensure that everyone shares the learning opportunity. (Buy these people business cards with their new title, or something...) Folks who disdain logs often develop a more mature attitude when it becomes their responsibility!

Keeping a Clean Machine

Nothing stays clean forever. You can clean your display screen with commercial cleaners intended for that purpose, but what about the rest of your system?

Heat is one of your computer's worst enemies. Most larger PCs have a fan to cool the power supply. Of course, if you have a laptop computer or a smaller PC, it may not have a fan. Computers with no fan won't accumulate internal dust and grit, so your main concern will be your keyboard.

If your unit has a fan, it probably is located at the rear of the machine. Check it occasionally to be sure it's actually running. A dead fan can overheat your PC and kill an expensive power supply or fixed disk!

If your unit has no fan, it still may have vents or slots to promote a flow of cool air. Avoid placing it in situations where the vents will be blocked.

The PC's other enemy is dirt. How clean is your computer? That fan can suck in a lot of very small grit and fluff which can cause random electrical errors and eventually even a major short-circuit. Many local companies now offer computer cleaning services. For a nominal fee they disassemble your PC and remove accumulations of dust and other material that may degrade your machine's cooling ability.

If your machine has a fan, inspect the grille. If it's clogged with dust, consider what the inside of the machine must be like and then get your PC cleaned promptly! Or follow the directions in the next section and clean it yourself. If you send it out, have the diskette drives tuned up at the same time. You also might ask them to clean any debris from beneath your keyboard keys, like spilled drink goop and crumbs. A small fee now will save large bills and lost data later!

All this advice also applies to your video monitor, but you always should have it cleaned by qualified professionals.

CAUTION

Video monitors contain high-voltage circuitry that can be dangerous, so don't open the monitor's case yourself!

Opening Your Computer's Case

The following is a general procedure for most PCs and PC clones. It does not apply to laptop, notebook, or portable computers. Those machines are more difficult to disassemble and seldom require internal maintenance.

Your computer's case is held shut by several (four or five) screws on the back, around the perimeter. Remove them, then gently lift or slide the cover from the base. Beware of tabs on the inside of the cover which may pull on the internal wiring! If the wiring catches on a tab, gently loosen it, then continue the removal.

See the manuals that came with your computer for more precise information. Many manuals tell you how to remove and replace your cover so that you can install additional circuit boards.

When you are ready to reassemble your PC, just reverse the way you opened it. Ensure that the cover fits neatly on the base and avoid pinching any wiring.

Removing Dust

You might think that a brush or a vacuum cleaner would be the best way to dust your computer, but an air hose is often better because the air stream dislodges dirt that a vacuum can miss. Some folks actually take their computers to a service station to blow the dust out. This is probably okay if you avoid directing strong blasts into the case.

If no air hose is available, you can use a vacuum cleaner with the hose attached to the output of the machine. In any case, avoid extremely strong air blasts which could dislodge the delicate components inside your PC.

CAUTION

Never work inside your computer with the AC power connected! Always disconnect it from the wall and also from all your other peripherals before servicing it!

TIP

Static electricity can damage your computer. Heed the warnings in your manuals.

TIP

*Moving streams
of air can generate
static electricity, so consider
cleaning your computer on a
rainy day; the humidity reduces
the static danger.*

How Often?

You should clean your computer whenever you notice a major accumulation of dust or fuzz on the fan grille. This might be as often as twice a year or as infrequently as never. It depends on the environment in which you use it and your personal habits. For example, if you accidentally spill a soft drink on the keyboard, you don't need to clean the entire machine but you should consider taking the keyboard in for service. The sugar in the soft drink will attract dust, which eventually will cause the keyboard to fail.

Backing Up Your Data

Most people put off backing up data until it's too late. Then they lose something important and the shock encourages them to develop better habits. To back up your files, you can use the DOS BACKUP and RESTORE commands or special software packages, or just develop some good, basic habits in the beginning.

Your hard drive probably has several subdirectories. There may be one for DOS, and many application programs generate their own during installation. Whenever possible, you should keep your data files or document files in separate subdirectories from the applications that use them. Then you can just back up the subdirectory without making another copy of the application software. Why make copies of it if you already have the distribution diskettes? You will find that backups happen faster on an orderly hard drive.

Why?

What did your computer cost? How much did you pay for your last application program? How long did it take to install it? What would you do if you lost all your files *right now!* Need we say more?

What?

You have a basic choice; you can back up only your data files or you can keep a copy of everything in your computer. Some fear-based people make several copies of everything, then spend time wondering which is the newest.

Like everyone else, I install application software on my computer, but I generally copy data files to diskettes as I use them. This gives me a second copy of all of my data with practically no effort, so I seldom do a full formal backup.

How?

Backing up your data can be as simple as making an extra copy of your file, or you can obtain special software and establish a rigorous schedule. If you decide to take the formal approach, consider using an aftermarket software package instead of the DOS BACKUP and RESTORE commands. The DOS commands are not popular because they are inefficient and troublesome. For example, it's difficult to locate and restore any one data file without restoring everything on the backup diskettes. This is a waste of time and can overwrite newer data on your hard disk.

Contact your retailer or your local PC users group to see what others in your area are doing. Sometimes you can learn a great deal from their experiences.

When?

Some companies establish a strict schedule for making backups, but individuals are usually far more cavalier about their schemes. There is even a National ANSI (American National Standards Institute) Standard, which sets forth a good regimen to follow.

In general, you should establish a schedule and a procedure—one that you can be comfortable with—then follow it. For example, when you install a new application, you may wish to copy the entire installation onto diskettes as a precaution, but you may do this only once. On the other hand, if you keep your financial information on your computer, you may wish to back it up every month, for safety.

Storing Your Backed-Up Data

Your diskette's enemies are heat, moisture, and magnetism. Always keep your important files away from these influences. You might also consider keeping them away from little fingers and the possibility of accidental damage!

Rearranging Your Data

In the last section we mentioned that you could usually store your data files in different subdirectories than the applications that use them. You control this arrangement when you use your computer. But there's also another, more fundamental way your data is organized which can affect your computer's performance. It involves the manner in which the data is written on your hard drive. You have no direct control over this, but you may benefit by some carefully chosen software utilities.

Recall that when you SAVE a file, DOS stores it wherever there's room on your disk. Your file appears to be located in one particular subdirectory, but in fact it may be scattered or fragmented in small pieces all over your disk. Fragmentation increases as you create and delete files because of the way DOS allocates disk space. Eventually you may notice that your computer takes a lot longer to open a large file (a spreadsheet, perhaps) than it once did.

Mechanical wear and tear is another problem you may encounter. When your disk drive is brand new, it's very precise, like the steering in a new car. Then after a few years, the mechanical parts inside your drive begin to wear and the drive is no longer as precise. It still can find your data most of the time, but it also may begin to generate occasional "sector not found" errors. These errors mean that the disk looked for your data but couldn't find it. The problem may be your drive's advancing age.

File fragmentation and drive wear (data misalignment) are bad because they increase the chance that DOS may lose some or all of a file. To avoid this problem, you should purchase special programs called disk maintenance utilities or disk defragmenters.

Disk defragmenters comb your disk drive and regroup your files for better, safer performance. The other utilities examine your hard drive and reposition the data very slightly, so that the drive has the best chance to find it every time. Obtain and use both of these utilities at least once each year to keep your drive in good health.

Glossary

Here are some common computer terms and their definitions.

ADDRESS   Computerese for a location, usually in memory. Just as your house has an address, computers locate almost everything they need by address.

ASCII (American Standard Code for Information Interchange)   The name for an official standard that defines a type of data format.

AUTOEXEC.BAT   A special DOS BATCH file usually found in the root drive of a computer system with a hard disk. This is an ASCII file containing special commands that the computer executes at boot. DOS always seeks this file during boot. If it finds the file in the root directory of your disk, it will execute the DOS commands contained within it.

BATCH files are ASCII files that contain a series of DOS commands, one per line. Batch filenames must always end with the .BAT extension. They are primarily a way to reduce the amount of typing we must do.

When you type the name of a batch file at the DOS prompt, DOS executes the commands in the file as if you had typed each of them in turn. You can use batch files to do repetitive tasks, call other batch files, or transfer control to other batch files. *See* BATCH FILES for more information.

The AUTOEXEC file provides a way to tailor your system to your personal needs. For example, you can use it to automatically install memory-resident programs, set your PROMPT, establish ENVIRON-MENTAL VARIABLES, and set your PATH. You can also use it to automatically start your favorite application each time you boot your PC.

Here's an example of an AUTOEXEC file. Yours will vary depending upon your hardware. Notice that entries preceded by double colons are ignored by DOS, so you can use them to include notes in the file. You could accomplish the same thing with the REM (remark) statement but I think it's more difficult to read. See CONFIG.SYS for a comparison.

```
@echo off
:: AUTOEXEC.BAT for my computer
:: Revised -
:: 21 Jun 92 - Created.

prompt $e[32m$p$g
path=\;c:\mouse;c:\utils;c:\dos50;c:\windows;
:: DOS environmental variables
set comspec=c:\dos50\command.com
:: mark the end of all envars
set last=envar
```

```
:: Memory-resident programs
loadhigh mouse /c2

:end
```

Although this is a simple batch file, they can be very complex. DOS offers a "batch file programming language" which many folks find intriguing. Of course, you should only have one file named AUTOEXEC.BAT in your system, but you can create other batch files with any name you wish.

If your computer has an AUTOEXEC.BAT file, it will be located in the root directory of your hard drive. This is a good file to backup onto a diskette and put in a safe place. If you lose it, your system will work quite differently, and you may have trouble remembering what was in it!

See your DOS manual for more information about Batch files, Batch file commands and the AUTOEXEC.BAT file.

BANG Tech-y slang for an exclamation point (!).

BATCH, BATCH FILE Text files that must be named with a .BAT extension. They contain a series of DOS commands, one per line, and allow you to run a batch of commands all at once. There is even a simple programming language you can use in your batch files. See your DOS manual for more information about these handy tools.

BAUD　An outdated term that refers to a specific company's serial communication scheme. The correct term is "Bits-Per-Second" or BPS, but you may see the two used interchangeably. *See* BPS.

BINARY ARITHMETIC　A type of arithmetic that has only two characters, zeros and ones. Binary arithmetic is handy for computers because electrical circuits have two states: on and off.

BIT　The smallest piece of information in a computer system. Collectively, eight bits make up one byte and two bytes make up one word.

BOOT, BOOTABLE　A generic term that refers to the way a computer turns on, the things it does to get ready for use. It's a shortened form of the old saying "to pull yourself up by the bootstraps."

BOOT DISKETTE, BOOTABLE DISKETTE　A diskette that has been formatted to include your Disk Operating System (DOS). Boot diskettes contain just enough programs to start your computer. They don't include special programs that you use in your work unless you put copies of those programs on the diskette.

BPS　Bits-Per-Second. A measure of the speed with which information is transferred over a serial communication link between two computers, or a computer and a peripheral. Often used interchangeably with the term BAUD, although the two measures are slightly different.

BUMP Tech-y slang for the times when the lights in your house dim, then brighten, or suddenly go out, then come back on, causin "power bump." These electrical surges are extremely hard on your computer's hardware and can also disrupt data or damage programs you are using at the time.

BYTE A unit of measure in the computer world. Generally, one byte is composed of eight bits. Two bytes comprise one word. Computer data is stored and handled in bytes or words.

CENTRONICS Another name for the parallel interface connector found on most printers today. Actually the name of a company that has produced a lot of printers over the years.

CONCATENATE A fancy way to say "hook them together." You can use the DOS COPY command to merge two files into one big file, a process called concatenation.

CONFIG.SYS A special DOS file. DOS always seeks this file during boot. If it finds the file in the root directory of your hard drive, it will execute the DOS statements contained within it. This file is similar in nature to the AUTOEXEC.BAT file, but the statements it contains use a different syntax, or rules, and it is not a batch file. At boot, DOS reads this file long before the AUTOEXEC.BAT file.

This file provides a way to automatically tie your hardware and software together. For example, you can use it to automatically install "device driver" programs, like "memory managers" and "video drivers." You can also use it to establish things DOS will need to know, like the number of files it can have open at one time.

Here's an example of a simple CONFIG.SYS file. Yours will vary depending upon your version of DOS, your hardware, the amount of RAM memory you have and the application programs you've installed. Notice that you can use the REM string to precede or "delimit" comments in this file, to keep track of your changes.

```
REM CONFIG.SYS for my computer
REM
REM Revised
REM 21 Jun 92 - Created.
REM These two devices MUST be listed first!
device=c:\dos50\himem.sys
dos=high,umb
REM Now the other stuff
devicehigh=c:\vgamax\fastbios.sys
devicehigh=c:\vgamax\eansi.sys
stacks=0,0
files=30
```

```
buffers=30
break=on
REM end of file
```

If your computer has a CONFIG.SYS file, it will be located in the root directory of your hard drive. This is a good file to backup onto a diskette and put in a safe place. If you lose it, your system will work quite differently, and you may have trouble remembering what was in it!

See your DOS manual for more information about device drivers and your CONFIG.SYS file.

CONFIGURATION   The process of setting up or initializing your software so that it and your hardware will work together.

CONVENTIONAL MEMORY   RAM memory addressed or "mapped" into the "conventional" memory area of your PC, also known as the "640K" (thousand byte) area of memory. You could say that the RAM memory in your computer is divided into neighborhoods, each with a specific purpose. The first or lowest 640K of RAM is used to run programs; it is the area in which DOS places a copy of any program you execute (unless you're using the DOS 5.0 LOADHIGH command to reposition it higher in memory).

CPU   This is an acronym for central processing unit. The term is from the days when computers occupied rooms or entire buildings.

Now we use the term computer to mean either the silicon microprocessor in a PC or a general reference to the PC and its case, not including the keyboard and other peripheral hardware.

DIRECTORY   A location on a disk. Also a listing of files in that location.

DISK   A disk is a data storage device, so called because it's round and thin like a pancake. Computer disks are available in several forms, with names like floppy diskettes and fixed or hard disks.

DISK DRIVE   An optional piece of hardware. Most computers need at least one to operate, and some PCs have many. Disk drives can be "hard," "fixed," or "floppy," referring to the type of disk the drive requires.

DISK OPERATING SYSTEM (DOS)   A special program that enables the computer to run. It is loaded from a disk (fixed or floppy) when the system is started or rebooted. If your PC is not bootable, you see error messages such as

> **Non-System disk or disk error**
> **Replace and press any key when ready**

or

> **Bad or missing Command Interpreter**

DISKETTE(S)   A diskette is a data storage device for your computer. Also known as floppy diskettes, floppy disks, or just floppies. Diskettes are made of material like the type used in audio cassettes and coated with a similar magnetic substance. Floppies are available in several sizes but the most common ones are 5$\frac{1}{4}$ inch and 3$\frac{1}{2}$ inch (diameter).

DOWNLOAD   To transfer a file from somewhere else, to your location. To receive a file. In telecommunications, to move a file from a remote source, like a bulletin board, to your computer.

EGA (ENHANCED GRAPHICS ADAPTOR)   A type of video system offering 640 x 350 resolution. Now replaced by VGA systems.

ENVIRONMENT VARIABLE (ENVAR)   The DOS way for programs to keep track of small but significant things that help them run faster and perform better or things that affect your computing environment.

EXPANDED MEMORY   Additional RAM memory installed in your PC and accessed by a technique called "bank switching" from a block of addresses above the lower 640K of "conventional" memory. Expanded memory is most useful in older PCs that do not use the Intel™ 80286 or higher microprocessors, the central processing unit or heart of your PC. Expanded memory is useful only if you are running a program that knows how to access it or applications that can communicate with this memory manager.

EXTENDED MEMORY   Additional RAM memory installed in your PC and "mapped" to addresses above the 1M (one million byte) boundary. Extended memory can only be installed in PCs that use the Intel™ 80286 or higher microprocessors. PCs with earlier microprocessors (the 8088 and 8086) are not capable of addressing (using) it at all.

FILE, FILENAMES   A way of storing information. Although you can refer to programs as files, most people use the word to mean data files, as opposed to programs. You generally can choose the filename (within limits) but your operating system sets the basic rules for file storage and retrieval, and your programs abide strictly by these rules. DOS has strict rules for filenames. They can be a single word, such as README, or they can have two parts, such as README.DOC. In either case, the first part can have no more than eight letters and the second, no more than three.

If the filename has two parts, they are in most cases separated by a period. Here's an instance where DOS is not perfect. When you type **dir** to see a listing of your files, the periods are not shown! Instead, you see columns of words and numbers, such as

GAMES	<DIR>	7-06-91	2:27p
UTILS	<DIR>	7-06-91	2:26p
AUTOEXEC BAT	4043	4-05-92	7:53p

CONFIG SYS	1045	4-05-92	7:52p
README	1024	4-07-92	9:52p
README DOC	1503	11-03-91	11:07p

DOS is cranky. We must learn that the file named CONFIG.SYS is displayed here as **CONFIG   SYS**. DOS makes us follow its rules but then violates those same rules with abandon!

FILTER   To reduce or eliminate data you don't want. This is a very handy way to locate just the file you're seeking quickly, or to restrict lists to manageable sizes on your screen.

FIXED DISK   A data storage device in your computer, usually permanently installed. Fixed disks are the most common type of bulk storage media in your computer. One fixed disk may be capable of storing up to several hundred megabytes (M) of information.

FIXED DRIVE   A type of data storage device. *See* FIXED DISK.

FLOPPY DISK   A type of data storage device. *See* DISKETTE.

FLOPPY DRIVE   The computer hardware that reads and writes a floppy diskette. *See* DISKETTE.

FONT   One complete collection of letters, punctuation marks, numbers, and special characters with a consistent typeface, weight (Roman or bold), posture (upright or italic), and size (height).

FOOTNETTING   *See* SNEAKERNETTING.

FORMAT, FORMATTING   A DOS program that furnishes the structure or format that is used to locate information on the disk. New hard disks and floppy diskettes are blank. When you format them, you have the option of creating a bootable diskette. *See also* DISK OPERATING SYSTEM (DOS).

FRAGMENTED, FRAGMENTATION   The state of your files when they are scattered all over your disk in tiny chunks. When you save a file, DOS stores it in the next available cubbyhole on your disk. If that cubbyhole won't hold the entire file, DOS puts some of it there and then seeks another cubbyhole, until the file is completely stored. Fragmentation slows your machine considerably when it's reading or writing to the hard drive, but this can be solved with a program called a defragmenter.

GLITCH   Tech-y slang for a mistake or an error.

HARD DISK, HARD DRIVE   Interchangeable names for a storage device that is like a floppy diskette but with more room. It typically is located inside your computer and is more fragile (and far more expensive) than a diskette.

HOTKEY   A combination of keystrokes. *See also* TSR (TERMINATE-AND-STAY-RESIDENT).

INTERLACE, INTERLACING   Video terms that refer to the way a picture is "painted" on your monitor.

INTERRUPT   The ability of a computer to handle chores that occur at unexpected times. You may encounter interrupts with names like IRQ3 and IRQ4 when setting up a serial port card or telecommunications software. In general, COM1 or COM3 should be assigned to IRQ4 (interrupt #4) and COM2 or COM4 should be paired with IRQ3 (interrupt #3).

These interrupts are actually a kind of address for programs that handle your serial ports. Most of the peripherals in your PC are serviced by interrupts, as shown in the following list, but the only ones you have to choose are those for the serial ports; the rest of them are chosen automatically:

IRQ0 = Timer

IRQ1 = Keyboard

IRQ2 = (reserved)

IRQ3 = COM2 (and COM4)

IRQ4 = COM1 (and COM3)

IRQ5 = (reserved)

IRQ6 = Floppy drive(s)

IRQ7 = Printer

IRQ   *See* INTERRUPT.

LED (LIGHT EMITTING DIODE)   A solid-state light source available in red, blue, green, orange, or yellow. They seldom wear out but they can become damaged and fail to illuminate. Replacement generally requires a technician.

MEMORY RESIDENT   A name for programs that, once called (executed), remains in memory until you reboot your computer, unless you specifically remove them. These programs can behave in many ways but their common feature is the tendency to remain active and occupy memory. The DOS PRINT command is an example of a memory-resident program. See *TSRs* for more information.

MICROPROCESSOR   The Central Processing Unit, or CPU, of your PC, contained on a microchip. The 80x86 family of microprocessors from Intel are at the core of IBM PCs and compatibles.

MODEM   Modems change computer signals to and from a structure that telephone lines can transmit. You can use a modem to communicate with another computer over the telephone lines if you have the appropriate software.

NONINTERLACED   *See* INTERLACE, INTERLACING.

OFF-LINE   *See* ON-LINE.

ON-LINE   Operating, turned on. Computers are on-line when they're operating and off-line when they're being maintained or not in use. Some printers do not respond to their own local keypads while they're paying attention to the computer. You must press a button on the printer's keypad to take it off-line before you can control it.

PARALLEL PORT   See PORTS.

PARITY   A simple error-checking scheme used in serial communications. Both ends must agree on the parity they will seek: odd or even (or none). Parity is an old scheme that's not very dependable.

PERIPHERAL   A catchall term for anything not actually enclosed in your computer's main case. Peripherals are usually added to the system as time and money allow. Some common peripherals are printers, modems, and joysticks.

PORTS   A doorway for data, either coming in or going out. Computer ports are either serial or parallel, depending on the way the data moves through the doorway. Data moves through a serial port more slowly than through a parallel port. Computer serial ports are called COM (COMmunication) ports, and are numbered beginning with 1.

RESOLUTION　A measure of the quality of a video display. Higher numbers generally mean better pictures. Early video displays could resolve only a few colors and they looked grainy. Newer units can resolve thousands of colors and produce beautifully clear, sharp pictures because they can produce many more dots on the screen than their predecessors. *See also* INTERLACE, INTERLACING.

ROOT, ROOT DIRECTORY　The first or most basic directory on a PC diskette or hard disk. For example, if your disk drive is A:, the root directory of any diskette in the drive will be A:\.

SCSI　"SCSI" (pronounced "SKUHZI") or "Small Computer System Interface." A special high-speed interface for disk drives and other peripherals.

SECTOR　A section of your disk used for storage. DOS divides your disk into pie-shaped wedges. You may get a "sector not found" error message, which can mean some data has been lost. *See also* FRAGMENTED, FRAGMENTATION.

SERIAL PORT　*See* PORTS.

SNEAKERNETTING　Tech-y slang for a method of moving data among computers. We put our data on a diskette and then walk it to another computer (wearing our sneakers).

SPLAT　Tech-y slang for the asterisk (*).

STOP BITS   The number of bits sent between bytes in a serial communication scheme. Used by the receiving computer to synchronize reception of serial information from the sender. Most computer links will require either one or two "stop bits."

SURGE PROTECTOR   An inexpensive device designed to absorb momentary AC power surges before they can damage your computer. *See also* UPS (UNINTERRUPTIBLE POWER SUPPLY).

SVGA (Super Video Graphics Array)   A type of video system offering up to 1024 x 768 resolution. One of the newer systems. *See also* VGA.

SYSTEM   One of those unfortunate, overused computer words, referring to either a collection of computer parts or to a certain kind of program your computer uses. A system diskette is one that contains DOS, a bootable diskette. A computer system generally includes the computer, a keyboard, a video monitor, a disk drive, a printer, and a power supply.

TOGGLE   The process of switching on, then off, then on, and so forth. Several keyboard keys are toggles because their function is either activated or deactivated with each press. Toggle also describes a software function that is alternately activated and deactivated with each call.

TSR (TERMINATE-AND-STAY-RESIDENT) A term used to refer to both a type of program and a method of installation. TSRs load themselves into memory, then terminate, but stay resident in memory so that you can call them up quickly with a special combination of keystrokes (a hotkey) while you're using another application.

The main advantage TSR programs offer is convenience, but they occupy memory and can conflict with other TSRs or certain applications. The only way to know for sure is to try them.

UNIX A different operating system than DOS, with different commands and syntax. Usually found on workstations and mainframe computers. Some companies now offer UNIX-like operating systems for personal computers.

UPLOAD To transfer a file from your location to somewhere else. To send a file. In telecommunications, to move a file from your computer to a remote destination, like a bulletin board.

UPS (UNINTERRUPTIBLE POWER SUPPLY) A special power supply connected between the wall and your PC. A UPS is designed to protect your computer from power surges and brownouts that can damage the delicate electronics in your computer or cause it to scramble your data. In some cases, such surges can even damage your hard disk. A UPS is generally necessary only in extreme cases — to protect medical equipment, or in a factory where the AC power is extremely unreliable.

VGA (Video Graphics Array)   A type of video system offering 640 x 480 resolution. This is presently the most common system, gradually being replaced by SVGA (Super VGA) and XGA.

VIRUS   A computer program that replicates itself by attaching to other programs and carrying out unwanted and sometimes damaging operations.

VOLATILE, VOLATILITY   A measure of data retention in data storage devices. RAM memory is very volatile because the data disappears when you remove power. Disk drives are less volatile because the data remains even without power (but can be changed by strong electromagnetic fields, such as those emitted by your monitor, an electric motor, or a refrigerator magnet). CD ROMS are probably the least volatile because their data cannot be changed easily.

WILDCARD   Characters used as a filter, usually to search through a file. Wildcards are the DOS equivalent of "Hey you!" because they can affect several files at once. There are two DOS wildcard characters: the question mark (?) and the asterisk (*)—also known as the splat. Also *see* FILTER.

WORD   A unit of measure in the computer world. Computer data is stored and handled in bytes or words. Generally, one word is composed of two bytes or sixteen bits.

XGA   IBM's newest video system, offering 1280 x 1024 resolution. Intended to replace SVGA systems.

Index